ANTHROPOLOGY AND COMMUNITY ACTION

Elizabeth Hegeman
and
Leonard Kooperman

Anchor Books
Anchor Press / Doubleday
Garden City, New York

Anchor Books Edition: 1974
ISBN: 0-385-08461-7
Library of Congress Catalog Card Number: 73–18908
Copyright © 1974 by Elizabeth Hegeman and Leonard Kooperman
Printed in the United States of America
First Edition

ACKNOWLEDGMENTS

We wish to thank our editor, Elizabeth Knappman, for her guidance and encouragement in the preparation of this book.

We wish to acknowledge those authors and publishers who kindly gave permission for the use of the selections reprinted in this book.

We thank those teachers and friends who have stimulated our interest in this area, and our friend Lillian Kagan for introducing us.

The order of the names on the title page was decided by the flip of a coin.

CONTENTS

FOREWORD

Many American social scientists have felt that cities cannot satisfy peoples' social needs as well as rural life does. Early studies of urbanism have attributed family disorganization, high divorce rates, and the breakdown of traditional values to city life. People widely believe that urban life imposes isolation and depersonalization: even city dwellers complain of the suspicion, unfriendliness, and anonymity they feel from other people, and notice in themselves.

If these qualities are really a necessary part of urban life, more and more people will be condemned to fragmented, disoriented existences as the world's urban population increases. There is little question that Western cities have failed in many ways to provide meaningful lives for their inhabitants. But some of the failures that have come to be associated with cities may in fact be due to outdated structures, rather than to the intrinsic properties of cities. The value of cities lies in proximity and economy for a large number of people, which can mean that individual options are increased and that groups can be formed based on choice rather than ascription.

Urban life combined with industrialization is the newest form of social life. Industrialization brings with it special problems—one is that the economies of scale that create a high standard of living depend upon large markets and the standardization of the demands of large numbers of people. People have to be treated uniformly to participate in a mass economy.

A second problem of industrialization is the centralization—perhaps overcentralization—of organizations designed to serve people. In the effort to deal with large numbers of people even-handedly, Americans have stressed centralization in the administering of services. In the early part of this century, governmental reform efforts endorsed pyramid-like hierarchies as a way of promoting efficiency, coordinating among agencies, and eliminating graft and corruption. Today we even have a trend toward super-agencies inspired by much the same philosophy.

However, in the zeal for efficiency, important aspects of urban populations have been ignored. Present-day cities are more heterogeneous ethnically and with respect to class than the reformers ever dreamed, and the great failure of a centralized bureaucracy is its inability to cope effectively with these diversities. In order for a centralized bureaucracy to function, it must assume that the people it serves can be dealt with uniformly, and develop sets of rules to that end. In the course of this process, administrative requirements may be met, but it is easy for service to the clients to recede in importance. When the goal of an agency is to enhance the quality of life, it is even more absurd to put the needs of the bureaucracy above the needs of the people. The regulation that dogs are not allowed in public housing is applied equally to the elderly and infirm in need of protection, in the interests of uniformity.

The philosophy of assimilation is closely related to that of centralization since highly centralized bureaucracies cannot adequately recognize differences. Qualitative differences such as ethnicity have to be translated into quantifiable ones: the Puerto Rican child who fails a spelling test may know how to spell in Spanish, but all the teacher can see is the number of errors. As a result, agencies are not meeting the needs of the people they were designed to serve—perhaps because they do not know what they are.

The recognition of cultural diversity and participation in decision-making processes are basic human rights. Since these are rights, they cannot be conferred as favors from the outside. City agencies must learn how to stimulate people to claim these rights, and then face the redefinition of their position. The recognition of cultural diversity does not mean putting the needs of any one minority group over the needs of another, nor does full participation in the decision-making process mean destruction of that process through the exclusion of the others who have the same rights. At present, paternalistic relationships emerge because agencies assume they know what to do—how and where to build "good" housing, what kind of curriculum schools should have—and proceed to provide it. When these policies are forced on urban dwellers, they become apathetic and dissatisfied, even if they would have chosen the same course of action if given the chance.

Alienation pervades many areas of modern life; the de-
r   .to workers in Ohio for more satisfaction than
;   e production offers is an example from industry
(   )pens when efficiency is valued above worker grati-
.   this book we present alternatives to the alienating
)s that develop as a result of overcentralization and
           m. In the kinds of societies anthropologists usually
           rsonal lives and community activity are fused—people
           it it matters whether they go to a meeting or not, but
city   wellers frequently do not even bother to vote.

Bureaucracies are notoriously static, ritualized, and resistant to change. A structure becomes outmoded when the emphasis is on record-keeping, going to conferences, and report-writing rather than on finding out what the people sitting on the wooden benches want. Structures are more likely to respond to pressures and demands from outside than they are likely to change from within, but even external pressures sometimes have to be as extreme as court actions and sit-ins.

Decentralization is often an important part of the philosophy of those who challenge bureaucratic structures to change. But decentralization is very threatening to bureaucrats—they accurately perceive it as a loss of power. In addition, it can cause divisiveness if local groups begin to fight with each other instead of fighting for mutual ends. If new facilities have to be built and staffed, new public funds must be found, which can become new sources of graft. Of all the problems decentralization brings, the overriding one is the illusion of change when the only difference is that new people are performing the old rituals. For example, for community control to be effective, minority group staffing is essential; but without real structural reform, the new staff can come to resemble the bureaucrats they were hired to replace.

The problem of defining "community" is a crucial one to the issue of community control. The absence of a sense of community in cities is isolating, and the spectator activities city life offers compensate only partly for the participation which is part of a feeling of community. Community does not have to be defined in strictly geographical terms—it can also mean groups of people with something in common, such as ex-convicts who have established a self-help organization.

Anthropology is unique among the social sciences in its focus on community. It attempts to describe what community is in as many different settings as there are, without imposing arbitrary definitions beforehand. The study of other cultures has many other applications to urban problems. Some of the pressing problems that confront us are so controversial that it is hard to fully understand them without a different perspective; the distance of cross-cultural examples keeps them from provoking intense loyalties and partisan commitments.

Anthropology assumes that the connections between behavior and feelings make sense. The field worker tries to look at the world from the point of view of the people he studies. Despite the romanticization of our rural past, as expressed in the popularity of denim, patchwork, and gingham clothing, most people who are concerned with urban problems have grown up in cities and suburbs, and have very little idea of what it can be like to live in a society with little specialization—the man who uses a weapon has cut down the tree from which it is made, and will have to butcher the animal he kills. In contrast, a city child is now given credit for saying that milk comes from bottles in the latest revision of a widely used intelligence test.

In a society where everyone knows everyone else, human contacts are individual and personal; they are continuous over long periods of time. These qualities could enhance social agencies in our cities. Anthropologists respect cultural differences in values and ways of living, and studying their work can show how varieties of values can be fulfilled rather than destroyed. Cities need structures that can take variety into account, and while anthropology cannot offer prescriptions for structural change, it shows us the value of variety.

Anthropology has documented the failure of paternalistic models of organization imposed from the outside, by studying and describing the results of colonialism. It has been an exceedingly difficult task for traditional societies to take Western structures and invest them with meaning. For example, the modern African bureaucrat is still expected by his extensive family to fulfill traditional obligations. His dilemma is that his family feels it has a right to the government resources he now has access to, but he cannot reconcile their demands with the requirements for impartiality of his civil service job. Highly centralized municipal bureaucracies parallel this failure by attempting to impose bureaucratic demands on people that contradict their cultural values and life styles. Colonialism at home has been no more successful than colonialism abroad. Even though funding for projects will usually have to come from outside the community, the initiative and the implementing of projects must rest with the community.

We do not advocate turning Manhattan into an island of hunters and gatherers—structures from one society cannot always be adopted into another. But the results of anthropological work provide some insights into what city dwellers have a right to demand and expect from urban life.

PART I
PROBLEMS IN CULTURAL COMMUNICATION

The job of the anthropologist, who tries to study cultures while changing them as little as possible, seems very different from the job of someone who works in a city hospital, a community agency, or an urban school system. These people want to change city life, whether by revamping the structure of an aftercare clinic, improving a school lunch program, or teaching a child to read.

But there are a number of similarities that make the experience of the anthropologist useful. Both types of work are with people of different backgrounds from the worker. Americans sometimes try to minimize these differences, preferring the "melting pot" myth, but in fact, cities are made up of a staggering variety of ethnic and class groups having different values and ways of doing things. Most community agencies are not set up to take into account these differences among clients, and so the burden of understanding and coping with them falls on the person who has contact with the public. It is difficult to mediate between two groups of people, the agency and the clients, who have two different sets of perceptions, vocabularies, and goals. The job of the person handling this two-way communication is more challenging than that of the anthropologist whose task is to make the culture he studies intelligible to his readers.

The anthropologist lives with the people he works with. Understanding the sources of the isolation and deprivation he experiences can help the person in the city deal with the same kinds of problems. The frustration of not meeting with acceptance and cooperation is easier to handle for someone who expects it. It may help to have satisfying contacts with people who understand him, and have the same goals and problems.

The position of the outsider who represents a city agency or a university is not initially clear to the people of the community. They may see him as more powerful than he really is, or they may see him as inconsequential. Seeming effective without seeming dangerous or generating resentment is a challenging task. The outsider has to work to make himself understood—care and attention will go into the creation of a role acceptable to both sides.

This role will differ according to the structure and expectations of the community. Lee was included by the Bushmen in their system of reciprocities; Chagnon on the other hand remained an object of extortion. Evans-Pritchard's role changed over the course of his field work as his inquiries came to be more fully accepted by the Nuer. The community mental health workers in Berlin's article knew they could not do their job by sitting in their offices; yet they would have lost their effectiveness if they had behaved like community members. They created a catalytic role by keeping in close touch with the community without becoming intrusive.

Introduction to
Beginning Field Work With the Nuer

Anthropological field work begins with the establishment of "rapport"—a mutually acceptable exchange, such as tobacco for kinship information, is necessary for communication to begin. This was difficult for Evans-Pritchard because the Nuer neither needed nor wanted him there. Among the Nuer, a cattle people of East Africa, no one takes orders, and so, in the absence of any strong incentive, the outsider is ignored. Evans-Pritchard's situation was more difficult than that of many field workers because he was dependent for his survival upon a group of people who had very little interest in him.

Given these conditions a great deal of persistence was required for Evans-Pritchard to complete his classic work. Over the course of six years he was finally accepted by the Nuer. He was supported during this time by the colonial government and by private foundations. Even when the object is to gather information without changing anything, a great deal of time and money are often required. Many of Evans-Pritchard's problems are similar to those found in the urban setting. An outsider in a community often faces the problem of wanting something from the community, without there being something of value he can offer in return. This makes it hard to establish a point from which communication can build. Short-term funding and limited commitment of time preclude the sustained involvement required for effective contact, whatever the goals.

Often the person working in an urban setting is a representative of a power structure or group toward which the community has learned to be antagonistic. Evans-Pritchard may not have been responsible for the actions of the colonial army, but as an Englishman he did have to cope with the consequences in the course of his field work. Similarly, the community health worker may be held responsible for the poor postal service, garbage collection, or school system in the community he is working with. It is important to know the history of contact with the community so that it can be taken into account.

Elsewhere in his work, Evans-Pritchard describes his difficulties in avoiding becoming identified with one conflicting faction or another among the Nuer. He needed to keep lines of communication open with as many different people as possible in order to gather accurate information. In order to be effective in the entire community, the urban worker must accept help in order to build relationships, while avoiding obligations to any special interest group.

---

1. BEGINNING FIELD WORK WITH THE NUER

by E. E. Evans-Pritchard

. . . I arrived in Nuerland early in 1930. Stormy weather prevented my luggage from joining me at Marseilles, and owing to errors, for which I was not responsible, my food stores were not forwarded from Malakal and my Zande servants were not instructed to meet me. I proceeded to Nuerland (Leek country) with my tent, some equipment, and a few stores bought at Malakal, and two servants, an Atwot and a Bellanda, picked up hastily at the same place.

When I landed at Yoahnyang on the Bahr el Ghazal the Catholic missionaries there showed me much kindness. I waited for nine days on the river bank for the carriers I had been promised. By the tenth day only four of them had arrived and if it had not been for the assistance of an Arab

From *The Nuer* by E. E. Evans-Pritchard, Oxford University Press, London, 1940, pp. 9–13.

merchant, who recruited some local women, I might have been delayed for an indefinite period.

On the following morning I set out for the neighbouring village of Pakur, where my carriers dropped tent and stores in the centre of a treeless plain, near some homesteads, and refused to bear them to the shade about half a mile further. Next day was devoted to erecting my tent and trying to persuade the Nuer, through my Atwot servant who spoke Nuer and some Arabic, to remove my abode to the vicinity of shade and water, which they refused to do. Fortunately a youth, Nhial, who has since been my constant companion in Nuerland, attached himself to me and after twelve days persuaded his kinsmen to carry my goods to the edge of the forest where they lived.

My servants, who, like most natives of the Southern Sudan, were terrified of the Nuer, had by this time become so scared that after several sleepless and apprehensive nights they bolted to the river to await the next steamer to Malakal, and I was left alone with Nhial. During this time the local Nuer would not lend a hand to assist me in anything and they only visited me to ask for tobacco, expressing displeasure when it was denied them. When I shot game to feed myself and my Zande servants, who had at last arrived, they took the animals and ate them in the bush, answering my remonstrances with the rejoinder that since the beasts had been killed on their land they had a right to them.

My main difficulty at this early stage was inability to converse freely with the Nuer. I had no interpreter. None of the Nuer spoke Arabic. There was no adequate grammar of the language and, apart from three short Nuer–English vocabularies, no dictionary. Consequently the whole of my first and a large part of my second expedition were taken up with trying to master the language sufficiently to make inquiries through it, and only those who have tried to learn a very difficult tongue without the aid of an interpreter and adequate literary guidance will fully appreciate the magnitude of the task.

After leaving Leek country I went with Nhial and my two Zande servants to Lou country. We motored to Muot dit with the intention of residing by the side of its lake, but found

it entirely deserted, for it was too early for the annual con-
centration there. When some Nuer were found they refused
to divulge the whereabouts of nearby camps and it was with
considerable difficulty that we located one. We pitched our
tents there and when the campers retired on Muot dit we
accompanied them.

My days at Muot dit were happy and remunerative. I made
friends with many Nuer youths who endeavoured to teach
me their language and to show me that if I was a stranger
they did not regard me as an obnoxious one. Every day I
spent hours fishing with these lads in the lake and conversing
with them in my tent. I began to feel my confidence returning
and would have remained at Muot dit had the political situation been more favourable. A Government force surrounded
our camp one morning at sunrise, searched for two prophets
who had been leaders in a recent revolt, took hostages, and
threatened to take many more if the prophets were not
handed over. I felt that I was in an equivocal position, since
such incidents might recur, and shortly afterwards returned
to my home in Zandeland, having accomplished only three
and a half months' work among the Nuer.

It would at any time have been difficult to do research
among the Nuer, and at the period of my visit they were
unusually hostile, for their recent defeat by Government
forces and the measures taken to ensure their final submission
had occasioned deep resentment. Nuer have often remarked
to me, "You raid us, yet you say we cannot raid the Dinka";
"You overcame us with firearms and we had only spears. If
we had had firearms we would have routed you"; and so forth.
When I entered a cattle camp it was not only as a stranger
but as an enemy, and they seldom tried to conceal their dis-
gust at my presence, refusing to answer my greetings and even
turning away when I addressed them.

At the end of my 1930 visit to Nuerland I had learnt a
little of the language but had the scantiest notes of their customs. In the dry season of 1931 I returned to make a fresh
attempt, going first for a fortnight to the American Mission
at Nasser, where I was generously assisted by the American
and Nuer staff, and then to cattle camps on the Nyanding
river—an unfortunate choice, for the Nuer there were more

hostile than those I had hitherto encountered and the conditions were harsher than any I had previously experienced. The water was scanty and foul, the cattle were dying of rinderpest, and the camps swarmed with flies. The Nuer would not carry my stores and equipment, and as I had only two donkeys, one of them lame, it was impossible to move. Eventually I managed to obtain a lorry and extricate myself, but not before experiencing the Nuer in his most paralysing mood. As every effort was made to prevent me from entering the cattle camps and it was seldom that I had visitors I was almost entirely cut off from communication with the people. My attempts to prosecute inquiries were persistently obstructed.

Nuer are expert at sabotaging an inquiry and until one has resided with them for some weeks they steadfastly stultify all efforts to elicit the simplest facts and to elucidate the most innocent practices. I have obtained in Zandeland more information in a few days than I obtained in Nuerland in as many weeks. After a while the people were prepared to visit me in my tent, to smoke my tobacco, and even to joke and make small talk, but they were unwilling either to receive me in their windscreens or to discuss serious matters. Questions about customs were blocked by a technique I can commend to natives who are inconvenienced by the curiosity of ethnologists. The following specimen of Nuer methods is the commencement of a conversation on the Nyanding river, on a subject which admits of some obscurity but, with willingness to co-operate, can soon be elucidated.

I: Who are you?
Cuol: A man.
I: What is your name?
Cuol: Do you want to know my *name*?
I: Yes.
Cuol: You want to know *my* name?
I: Yes, you have come to visit me in my tent and I would like to know who you are.
Cuol: All right. I am Cuol. What is your name?
I: My name is Pritchard.
Cuol: What is your father's name?

I: My father's name is also Pritchard.

Cuol: No, that cannot be true. You cannot have the same name as your father.

I: It is the name of my lineage. What is the name of your lineage?

Cuol: Do you want to know the name of my lineage?

I: Yes.

Cuol: What will you do with it if I tell you? Will you take it to your country?

I: I don't want to do anything with it. I just want to know it since I am living at your camp.

Cuol: Oh well, we are Lou.

I: I did not ask you the name of your tribe. I know that. I am asking you the name of your lineage.

Cuol: Why do you want to know the name of my lineage?

I: I don't want to know it.

Cuol: Then why do you ask me for it? Give me some tobacco.

I defy the most patient ethnologist to make headway against this kind of opposition. One is just driven crazy by it. Indeed, after a few weeks of associating solely with Nuer one displays, if the pun be allowed, the most evident symptoms of "Nuerosis." . . .

Introduction to
Doing Field Work Among the Yąnomamö

Many of the issues Chagnon faced in his field work crop up, in modified form, for someone working in a city. He had to lower his standards of cleanliness and change his eating habits; when working in the urban community, a person may be expected to accept conditions that may not be up to his standards in order to begin a social relationship. Chagnon felt lonely and needed companionship from the Yąnomamö of the Amazonian regions of Venezuela, and was disappointed when they tried to exploit him instead. He was forced to recognize how unrealistic it was for him to expect the Yąnomamö to place loyalty to him above survival or material advantage. In much the same way someone working in a city has to sort out his own unrealistic expectations of appreciation, gratitude, or acceptance from people who may not even understand what he is doing there. One solution rarely available to the anthropologist is to fall back on such reference groups as co-workers, friends, and family for support and approval that may not be initially forthcoming from the community.

Just as Chagnon had control over steel tools, the representative of an outside agency frequently exercises control over resources desirable to the people of a community and is likely to undergo some sort of testing. The power he has may even be exaggerated by people who see themselves as powerless; his inability to supply them with what they want can become a source of resentment because it is seen as a refusal to meet their needs. Here again, someone whose goals for the community involve change has an opportunity not available to the anthropologist: he can give meaning to his presence by explaining why he is there and enlist the community's cooperation on its own behalf. As people begin to understand his position more clearly, their resentment of his apparent power and control will be diminished, and they will feel more powerful themselves.

2. DOING FIELD WORK AMONG THE YĄNOMAMÖ

by Napoleon Chagnon

. . . We arrived at the village, Bisaasi-teri, about 2 P.M. and docked the boat along the muddy bank at the terminus of the path used by the Indians to fetch their drinking water. It was hot and muggy, and my clothing was soaked with perspiration. It clung uncomfortably to my body, as it did thereafter for the remainder of the work. The small, biting gnats were out in astronomical numbers, for it was the beginning of the dry season. My face and hands were swollen from the venom of their numerous stings. In just a few moments I was to meet my first Yąnomamö, my first primitive man. What would it be like? I had visions of entering the village and seeing 125 social facts running about calling each other kinship terms and sharing food, each waiting and anxious to have me collect his genealogy. I would wear them out in turn. Would they like me? This was important to me; I wanted them to be so fond of me that they would adopt me into their kinship system and way of life, because I had heard that successful anthropologists always get adopted by their people. I had learned during my seven years of anthropological training at the University of Michigan that kinship was equivalent to society in primitive tribes and that it was a moral way of life, "moral" being something "good" and "desirable." I was

From Yąnomamö: The Fierce People by Napoleon Chagnon, Holt, Rinehart & Winston, New York, 1968, pp. 4–11.

determined to work my way into their moral system of kinship and become a member of their society.

My heart began to pound as we approached the village and heard the buzz of activity within the circular compound. Mr. Barker commented that he was anxious to see if any changes had taken place while he was away and wondered how many of them had died during his absence. I felt into my back pocket to make sure that my notebook was still there and felt personally more secure when I touched it. Otherwise, I would not have known what to do with my hands.

The entrance to the village was covered over with brush and dry palm leaves. We pushed them aside to expose the low opening to the village. The excitement of meeting my first Indians was almost unbearable as I duck-waddled through the low passage into the village clearing.

I looked up and gasped when I saw a dozen burly, naked, filthy, hideous men staring at us down the shafts of their drawn arrows! Immense wads of green tobacco were stuck between their lower teeth and lips making them look even more hideous, and strands of dark-green slime dripped or hung from their noses. We arrived at the village while the men were blowing a hallucinogenic drug up their noses. One of the side effects of the drug is a runny nose. The mucus is always saturated with the green powder and the Indians usually let it run freely from their nostrils. My next discovery was that there were a dozen or so vicious, underfed dogs snapping at my legs, circling me as if I were going to be their next meal. I just stood there holding my notebook, helpless and pathetic. Then the stench of the decaying vegetation and filth struck me and I almost got sick. I was horrified. What sort of a welcome was this for the person who came here to live with you and learn your way of life, to become friends with you? They put their weapons down when they recognized Barker and returned to their chanting, keeping a nervous eye on the village entrances.

We had arrived just after a serious fight. Seven women had been abducted the day before by a neighboring group, and the local men and their guests had just that morning recovered five of them in a brutal club fight that nearly ended in a shooting war. The abductors, angry because they lost five of the seven captives, vowed to raid the Bisaasi-teri. When we arrived and entered the village unexpectedly, the Indians feared that we were the raiders. On several occasions during the next two hours the men in the village jumped to their feet, armed themselves, and waited nervously for the noise outside the village to be identified. My enthusiasm for collecting ethnographic curiosities diminished in proportion to the number of times such an alarm was raised. In fact, I was relieved when Mr. Barker suggested that we sleep across the river for the evening. It would be safer over there.

As we walked down the path to the boat, I pondered the wisdom of having decided to spend a year and a half with this tribe before I had even seen what they were like. I am not ashamed to admit, either, that had there been a diplomatic way out, I would have ended my field work then and there. I did not look forward to the next day when I would be left alone with the Indians; I did not speak a word of their language, and they were decidedly different from what I had imagined them to be. The whole situation was depressing, and I wondered why I ever decided to switch from civil engineering to anthropology in the first place. I had not eaten all day, I was soaking wet from perspiration, the gnats were biting me, and I was covered with red pigment, the result of a dozen or so complete examinations I had been given by as many burly Indians. These examinations capped an otherwise grim day. The Indians would blow their noses into their hands, flick as much of the mucus off that would separate in a snap of the wrist, wipe the residue into their hair, and then carefully examine my face, arms, legs, hair, and the contents of my pockets. I asked Mr. Barker how to say "Your hands are dirty"; my comments were met by the Indians in the following way: They would "clean" their hands by spitting a quantity of slimy tobacco juice into them, rub them together, and then proceed with the examination.

Mr. Barker and I crossed the river and slung our hammocks. When he pulled his hammock out of a rubber bag, a heavy, disagreeable odor of mildewed cotton came with it. "Even the missionaries are filthy," I thought to myself. Within two weeks, everything I owned smelled the same way, and I lived with that odor for the remainder of the field work. My own habits of personal cleanliness reached such levels that I didn't even mind being examined by the Indians, as I was not much cleaner than they were after I had adjusted to the circumstances.

So much for my discovery that primitive man is not the picture of nobility and sanitation I had conceived him to be. I soon discovered that it was an enormously time-consuming task to maintain my own body in the manner to which it had grown accustomed in the relatively antiseptic environment of the northern United States. Either I could be relatively well fed and relatively comfortable in a fresh change of clothes and do very little field work, or, I could do considerably more field work and be less well fed and less comfortable.

It is appalling how complicated it can be to make oatmeal in the jungle. First, I had to make two trips to the river to haul the water. Next, I had to prime my kerosene stove with alcohol and get it burning, a tricky procedure when you are trying to mix powdered milk and fill a coffee pot at the same time: the alcohol prime always burned out before I could turn the kerosene on, and I would have to start all over. Or, I would turn the kerosene on, hoping that the element was still hot enough to vaporize the fuel, and start a small fire in my palm-thatched hut as the liquid kerosene squirted all over the table and walls and ignited. It was safer to start over with the alcohol. Then I had to boil the oatmeal and pick the bugs out of it. All my supplies, of course, were carefully stored in Indian-proof, rat-proof, moisture-proof, and insect-proof containers, not one of which ever served its purpose adequately. Just taking things out of the multiplicity of containers and repacking them afterward was a minor project in itself. By the time I had hauled the water to cook with, unpacked my food, prepared the oatmeal, milk, and coffee, heated water for dishes, washed and dried the dishes, repacked the food in the containers, stored the containers in locked trunks and cleaned up my mess, the ceremony of preparing breakfast had brought me almost up to lunch time!

Eating three meals a day was out of the question. I solved the problem by eating a single meal that could be prepared in a single container, or, at most, in two containers, washed my dishes only when there were no clean ones left, using cold river water, and wore each change of clothing at least a week to cut down on my laundry problem, a courageous undertaking in the tropics. I was also less concerned about sharing my provisions with the rats, insects, Indians, and the elements, thereby eliminating the need for my complicated storage process. I was able to last most of the day on *café con leche*, heavily sugared espresso coffee diluted about five to one with hot milk. I would prepare this in the evening and store it in a thermos. Frequently, my single meal was no more complicated than a can of sardines and a package of crackers. But at least two or three times a week I would do something sophisticated, like make oatmeal or boil rice and add a can of tuna fish or tomato paste to it. I even saved time by devising a water system that obviated the trips to the river. I had a few sheets of zinc roofing brought in and made a rain-water trap; I caught the water on the zinc surface, funneled it into an empty gasoline drum, and then ran a plastic hose from the drum to my hut. When the drum was exhausted in the dry season, I hired the Indians to fill it with water from the river.

I ate much less when I traveled with the Indians to visit other villages. Most of the time my travel diet consisted of roasted or boiled green plantains that I obtained from the Indians, but I always carried a few cans of sardines with me in case I got lost or stayed away longer than I had planned. I found peanut butter and crackers a very nourishing food, and a simple one to prepare on trips. It was nutritious and portable, and only one tool was required to prepare the meal, a hunting knife that could be cleaned by wiping the blade on a leaf. More importantly, it was one of the few foods the Indians would let me eat in relative peace. It looked too much like animal feces to them to excite their appetites.

I once referred to the peanut butter as the dung of cattle. They found this quite repugnant. They did not know what "cattle" were, but were generally aware that I ate several canned products of such an animal. I perpetrated this myth, if for no other reason than to have some peace of mind while I ate. Field workers develop strange defense mechanisms, and this was one of my own forms of adaptation. On another occasion I was eating a can of frankfurters and growing very weary of the demands of one of my guests for a share in my meal. When he asked me what I was eating, I replied: "Beef." He then asked, "What part of the animal are you eating?" to which I replied, "Guess!" He stopped asking for a share.

Meals were a problem in another way. Food sharing is important to the Yąnomamö in the context of displaying friendship. "I am hungry," is almost a form of greeting with them. I could not possibly have brought enough food with me to feed the entire village, yet they seemed not to understand this. All they could see was that I did not share my food with them at each and every meal. Nor could I enter into their system of reciprocities with respect to food; every time one of them gave me something "freely," he would dog me for months to pay him back, not with food, but with steel tools. Thus, if I accepted a plantain from someone in a different village while I was on a visit, he would most likely visit me in the future and demand a machete as payment for the time that he "fed" me. I usually reacted to these kinds of demands by giving a banana, the customary reciprocity in their culture—food for food—but this would be a disappointment for the individual who had visions of that single plantain growing into a machete over time.

Despite the fact that most of them knew I would not share my food with them at their request, some of them always showed up at my hut during mealtime. I gradually became accustomed to this and learned to ignore their persistent demands while I ate. Some of them would get angry because I failed to give in, but most of them accepted it as just a peculiarity of the subhuman foreigner. When I did give in, my hut quickly filled with Indians, each demanding a sample of the food that I had given one of them. If I did not give all a share, I was that much more despicable in their eyes.

A few of them went out of their way to make my meals unpleasant, to spite me for not sharing; for example, one man arrived and watched me eat a cracker with honey on it. He immediately recognized the honey, a particularly esteemed Yąnomamö food. He knew that I would not share my tiny bottle and that it would be futile to ask. Instead, he glared at me and queried icily, "Shaki! What kind of animal semen are you eating on that cracker?" His question had the desired effect, and my meal ended.

Finally, there was the problem of being lonely and separated from your own kind, especially your family. I tried to overcome this by seeking personal friendships among the Indians. This only complicated the matter because all my friends simply used my confidence to gain privileged access to my cache of steel tools and trade goods, and looted me. I would be bitterly disappointed that my "friend" thought no more of me than to finesse our relationship exclusively with the intention of getting at my locked up possessions, and my depression would hit new lows every time I discovered this. The loss of the possession bothered me much less than the shock that I was, as far as most of them were concerned, nothing more than a source of desirable items; no holds were barred in relieving me of these, since I was considered something subhuman, a non-Yąnomamö.

The thing that bothered me most was the incessant, passioned, and aggressive demands the Indians made. It would become so unbearable that I would have to lock myself in my mud hut every once in a while just to escape from it: Privacy is one of Western culture's greatest achievements. But I did not want privacy for its own sake; rather, I simply had to get away from the begging. Day and night for the entire time I lived with the Yąnomamö I was plagued by such demands as: "Give me a knife, I am poor!"; "If you don't take me with you on your next trip to Widokaiya-teri I'll chop a hole in your canoe!"; "Don't point your camera at me or I'll hit you!"; "Share your food with me!"; "Take me across the river in your canoe and be quick about it!"; "Give me a cooking pot!"; "Loan me your flashlight so I can go hunting tonight!"; "Give me medicine . . . I itch all over!"; "Take us on a week-long hunting trip with your shotgun!"; and "Give me an axe or I'll break into your hut when you are away visiting and steal one!" And so I was bombarded by such demands day after day, months on end, until I could not bear to see an Indian.

It was not as difficult to become calloused to the incessant begging as it was to ignore the sense of urgency, the impassioned tone of voice, or the intimidation and aggression with which the demands were made. It was likewise difficult to adjust to the fact that the Yąnomamö refused to accept "no" for an answer until or unless it seethed with passion and intimidation—which it did after six months. Giving in to a demand always established a new threshold; the next demand would be for a bigger item or favor, and the anger of the Indians even greater if the demand was not met. I soon learned that I had to become very much like the Yąnomamö to be able to get along with them on their terms: sly, aggressive, and intimidating.

Had I failed to adjust in this fashion I would have lost six months of supplies to them in a single day or would have spent most of my time ferrying them around in my canoe or hunting for them. As it was, I did spend a considerable amount of time doing these things and did succumb to their outrageous demands for axes and machetes, at least at first. More importantly, had I failed to demonstrate that I could not be pushed around beyond a certain point, I would have been the subject of far more ridicule, theft, and practical jokes than was the actual case. In short, I had to acquire a certain proficiency in their kind of interpersonal politics and to learn how to imply subtly that certain potentially undesirable consequences might follow if they did such and such to me. They do this to each other in order to establish precisely the point at which they cannot goad an individual any further without precipitating retaliation. As soon as I caught on to this and realized that much of their aggression was stimulated by their desire to discover my flash point, I got along much better with them and regained some lost ground. It was sort of like a political game that everyone played, but one in which each individual sooner or later had to display some sign that his bluffs and implied threats could be backed up. I suspect that the frequency of wife beating is a component of this syndrome, since men can display their ferocity and show others that they are capable of violence. Beating a wife with a club is considered to be an acceptable way of displaying ferocity and one that does not expose the male to much danger. The important thing is that the man has displayed his potential for violence and the implication is that other men better treat him with respect and caution.

After six months, the level of demand was tolerable in the village I used for my headquarters. The Indians and I adjusted to each other and knew what to expect with regard to demands on their part for goods, favors, and services. Had I confined my field work to just that village alone, the field experience would have been far more enjoyable. But, as I was interested in the demographic pattern and social organization of a much larger area, I made regular trips to some dozen different villages in order to collect genealogies or to recheck those I already had. Hence, the intensity of begging and intimidation was fairly constant for the duration of the field work. I had to establish my position in some sort of pecking order of ferocity at each and every village.

For the most part, my own "fierceness" took the form of shouting back at the Yąnomamö as loudly and as passionately as they shouted at me, especially at first, when I did not know much of their language. As I became more proficient in their language and learned more about their political tactics, I became more sophisticated in the art of bluffing. For example, I paid one young man a machete to cut palm trees and make boards from the wood. I used these to fashion a platform in the bottom of my dugout canoe to keep my possessions dry when I traveled by river. That afternoon I was doing informant work in the village; the long-awaited mission supply boat arrived, and most of the Indians ran out of the village to beg goods from the crew. I continued to work in the village for another hour or so and went down to the river to say "hello" to the men on the supply boat. I was angry when I discovered that the Indians had chopped up all my palm boards and used them to paddle their own canoes across the river. I knew that if I overlooked this incident I would have invited them to take even greater liberties with my goods in the future. I crossed the river, docked amidst their dugouts, and shouted for the Indians to come out and see me. A few of the culprits appeared, mischievous grins on their faces. I gave a spirited lecture about how hard I had worked to put those boards in my canoe, how I had paid a machete for the wood, and how angry I was that they destroyed my work in their haste to cross the river. I then pulled out my hunting knife and, while their grins disappeared, cut each of their canoes loose, set it into the current, and let them float away. I left without further ado and without looking back.

They managed to borrow another canoe and, after some effort, recovered their dugouts. The headman of the village later told me with an approving chuckle that I had done the correct thing. Everyone in the village, except, of course, the culprits, supported and defended my action. This raised my status.

Whenever I took such action and defended my rights, I got along much better with the Yąnomamö. A good deal of their behavior toward me was directed with the forethought of establishing the point at which I would react defensively. Many of them later reminisced about the early days of my work when I was "timid" and a little afraid of them, and they could bully me into giving goods away.

Theft was the most persistent situation that required me to take some sort of defensive action. I simply could not keep everything I owned locked in trunks, and the Indians came into my hut and left at will. I developed a very effective means for recovering almost all the stolen items. I would simply ask a child who took the item and then take that person's hammock when he was not around, giving a spirited lecture to the others as I marched away in a faked rage with the thief's hammock. Nobody ever attempted to stop me from doing this, and almost all of them told me that my technique for recovering my possessions was admirable. By nightfall the thief would either appear with the stolen object or send it along with someone else to make an exchange. The others would heckle him for getting caught and being forced to return the item.

With respect to collecting the data I sought, there was a very frustrating problem. Primitive social organization is kinship organization, and to understand the Yąnomamö way of life I had to collect extensive genealogies. I could not have deliberately picked a more difficult group to work with in this regard: They have very stringent name taboos. They attempt to name people in such a way that when the person dies and they can no longer use his name, the loss of the word in the language is not inconvenient. Hence, they name people for specific and minute parts of things, such as "toenail of some rodent," thereby being able to retain the words "toenail" and "(specific) rodent," but not being able to refer directly to the toenail of that rodent. The taboo is maintained even for the living: One mark of prestige is the courtesy others show you by not using your name. The sanctions behind the taboo seem to be an unusual combination of fear and respect.

I tried to use kinship terms to collect genealogies at first, but the kinship terms were so ambiguous that I ultimately had to resort to names. They were quick to grasp that I was bound to learn everybody's name and reacted, without my knowing it, by inventing false names for everybody in the village. After having spent several months collecting names and learning them, this came as a disappointment to me: I could not cross-check the genealogies with other informants from distant villages.

They enjoyed watching me learn these names. I assumed, wrongly, that I would get the truth to each question and that I would get the best information by working in public. This set the stage for converting a serious project into a farce. Each informant tried to outdo his peers by inventing a name even more ridiculous than what I had been given earlier, or by asserting that the individual about whom I inquired was married to his mother or daughter, and the like. I would have the informant whisper the name of the individual in my ear, noting that he was the father of such and such a child. Everybody would then insist that I repeat the name aloud, roaring in hysterics as I clumsily pronounced the name. I assumed that the laughter was in response to the violation of the name taboo or to my pronunciation. This was a reasonable interpretation, since the individual whose name I said aloud invariably became angry. After I learned what some of the names meant, I began to understand what the laughter was all about. A few of the more colorful examples are: "hairy vagina," "long penis," "feces of the harpy eagle," and "dirty rectum." No wonder the victims were angry. . . .

Introduction to
Eating Christmas in the Kalahari

Although some kind of mutually acceptable exchange must occur for field work to proceed, the anthropologist usually finds himself in the position of receiving much more than he gives. One of the stresses of field work is the guilt generated by enjoying greater comforts than the people with whom you are dealing. Richard Lee describes how his own emotional needs interfered with his professional task: the accurate perception and description of the mechanisms of Bushman reciprocity. After a year of field work, he was being treated as any Bushman would treat any other Bushman, yet because of his need to compensate for what they had given him, he needed to have his gift recognized on a grander scale than the values of Bushman society would allow.

Since the Bushmen live under the difficult conditions of the Kalahari, the habitual "put down" of the person who brings home the bacon serves as an insurance policy for the interdependence and the egalitarianism so fundamental to their culture. They succeeded in teaching him the humility essential for their own survival. Without his honesty with himself and his sense of humor, he might never have reached this important realization.

Someone working with people who have very limited resources in an urban setting can experience similar feelings to Lee's. Anthropologists are in the equivocal position of being there to investigate and not to help. The goals are different in the urban setting, but the main dilemma of how to use the limited resources in the face of overwhelming deprivations is the same. Should time and money be spent meeting the needs of a few people for urgent medical care or food, or is it more useful in the long run to plan basic changes, do publicity, and mobilize the larger community? The danger is that perceptions of priorities can be distorted by guilt. Stressful as this conflict may be, an awareness of it can keep the focus on effective action rather than charity.

Lee managed to use his own emotional reactions to gain an enriched perception of Bushman values. Coming from a culture where self-esteem is based on recognition of individual achievement, it was hard for him to suspend his own needs in order to see how a more collective culture worked. Since he has a similar need for recognition, the urban worker may have to examine his own motives frequently in order to gain the strength to relinquish it gracefully.

---

3. EATING CHRISTMAS IN THE KALAHARI

by Richard Borshay Lee

The !Kung Bushmen's knowledge of Christmas is thirdhand. The London Missionary Society brought the holiday to the southern Tswana tribes in the early nineteenth century. Later, native catechists spread the idea far and wide among the Bantu-speaking pastoralists, even in the remotest corners of the Kalahari Desert. The Bushmen's idea of the Christmas story, stripped to its essentials, is "praise the birth of white man's god-chief," what keeps their interest in the holiday high is the Tswana-Herero custom of slaughtering an ox for his Bushmen neighbors as an annual goodwill gesture. Since the 1930s, part of the Bushmen's annual round of activities has included a December congregation at the cattle posts for trading, marriage brokering, and several days of trance-dance feasting at which the local Tswana headman is host.

As a social anthropologist working with !Kung Bushmen, I found that the Christmas ox custom suited my purposes. I

From *Natural History Magazine*, 78 (December 1969), pp. 14–63.

had come to the Kalahari to study the hunting and gathering subsistence economy of the !Kung, and to accomplish this it was essential not to provide them with food, share my own food, or interfere in any way with their food-gathering activities. While liberal handouts of tobacco and medical supplies were appreciated, they were scarcely adequate to erase the glaring disparity in wealth between the anthropologist, who maintained a two-month inventory of canned goods, and the Bushmen, who rarely had a day's supply of food on hand. My approach, while paying off in terms of data, left me open to frequent accusations of stinginess and hard-heartedness. By their lights, I was a miser.

The Christmas ox was to be my way of saying thank you for the cooperation of the past year; and since it was to be our last Christmas in the field, I determined to slaughter the largest, meatiest ox that money could buy, insuring that the feast and trance dance would be a success.

Through December I kept my eyes open at the wells as the cattle were brought down for watering. Several animals were offered, but none had quite the grossness that I had in mind. Then, ten days before the holiday, a Herero friend led an ox of astonishing size and mass up to our camp. It was solid black, stood five feet high at the shoulder, had a five-foot span of horns, and must have weighed 1,200 pounds on the hoof. Food consumption calculations are my specialty, and I quickly figured that bones and viscera aside, there was enough meat —at least four pounds—for every man, woman, and child of the 150 Bushmen in the vicinity of /ai/ai who were expected at the feast.

Having found the right animal at last, I paid the Herero £20 ($56) and asked him to keep the beast with his herd until Christmas day. The next morning word spread among the people that the big solid black one was the ox chosen by /ontah (my Bushman name; it means, roughly, "whitey") for the Christmas feast. That afternoon I received the first delegation. Ben!a, an outspoken sixty-year-old mother of five, came to the point slowly.

"Where were you planning to eat Christmas?"

"Right here at /ai/ai," I replied.

"Alone or with others?"

"I expect to invite all the people to eat Christmas with me."

"Eat what?"

"I have purchased Yehave's black ox, and I am going to slaughter and cook it."

"That's what we were told at the well but refused to believe it until we heard it from yourself."

"Well, it's the black one," I replied expansively, although wondering what she was driving at.

"Oh, no!" Ben!a groaned, turning to her group. "They were right." Turning back to me she asked, "Do you expect us to eat that bag of bones?"

"Bag of bones! It's the biggest ox at /ai/ai."

"Big, yes, but old. And thin. Everybody knows there's no meat on that old ox. What did you expect us to eat off it, the horns?"

Everybody chuckled at Ben!a's one-liner as they walked away, but all I could manage was a weak grin.

That evening it was the turn of the young men. They came to sit at our evening fire. /gaugo, about my age, spoke to me man-to-man.

"/ontah, you have always been square with us," he lied. "What has happened to change your heart? That sack of guts and bones of Yehave's will hardly feed one camp, let alone all the Bushmen around /ai/ai." And he proceeded to enumerate the seven camps in the /ai/ai vicinity, family by family. "Perhaps you have forgotten that we are not few, but many. Or are you too blind to tell the difference between a proper cow and an old wreck? That ox is thin to the point of death."

"Look, you guys," I retorted, "that is a beautiful animal, and I'm sure you will eat it with pleasure at Christmas."

"Of course we will eat it; it's food. But it won't fill us up to the point where we will have enough strength to dance. We will eat and go home to bed with stomachs rumbling."

That night as we turned in, I asked my wife, Nancy: "What did you think of the black ox?"

"It looked enormous to me. Why?"

"Well, about eight different people have told me I got gypped; that the ox is nothing but bones."

"What's the angle?" Nancy asked. "Did they have a better one to sell?"

"No, they just said that it was going to be a grim Christmas because there won't be enough meat to go around. Maybe I'll get an independent judge to look at the beast in the morning."

Bright and early, Halingisi, a Tswana cattle owner, appeared at our camp. But before I could ask him to give me his opinion on Yehave's black ox, he gave me the eye signal that indicated a confidential chat. We left the camp and sat down.

"/ontah, I'm surprised at you; you've lived here for three years and still haven't learned anything about cattle."

"But what else can a person do but choose the biggest, strongest animal one can find?" I retorted.

"Look, just because an animal is big doesn't mean that it has plenty of meat on it. The black one was a beauty when it was younger, but now it is thin to the point of death."

"Well I've already bought it. What can I do at this stage?"

"Bought it already? I thought you were just considering it. Well, you'll have to kill it and serve it, I suppose. But don't expect much of a dance to follow."

My spirits dropped rapidly. I could believe that Ben!a and /gaugo just might be putting me on about the black ox, but Halingisi seemed to be an impartial critic. I went around that day feeling as though I had bought a lemon of a used car.

In the afternoon it was Tomazo's turn. Tomazo is a fine hunter, a top trance performer, and one of my most reliable informants. He approached the subject of the Christmas cow as part of my continuing Bushmen education.

"My friend, the way it is with us Bushmen," he began, "is that we love meat. And even more than that, we love fat. When we hunt we always search for the fat ones, the ones dripping with layers of white fat: fat that turns into a clear, thick oil in the cooking pot, fat that slides down your gullet, fills your stomach and gives you a roaring diarrhea," he rhapsodized.

"So, feeling as we do," he continued, "it gives us pain to be served such a scrawny thing as Yehave's black ox. It is big, yes, and no doubt its giant bones are good for soup, but fat is what we really crave and so we will eat Christmas this year with a heavy heart."

The prospect of a gloomy Christmas now had me worried, so I asked Tomazo what I could do about it.

"Look for a fat one, a young one . . . smaller, but fat. Fat enough to make us //gom ('evacuate the bowels'), then we will be happy."

My suspicions were aroused when Tomazo said that he happened to know of a young, fat, barren cow that the owner was willing to part with. Was Toma working on commission, I wondered? But I dispelled this unworthy thought when we approached the Herero owner of the cow in question and found that he had decided not to sell.

The scrawny wreck of a Christmas ox now became the talk of the /ai/ai water hole and was the first news told to the outlying groups as they began to come in from the bush for the feast. What finally convinced me that real trouble might be brewing was the visit from u!au, an old conservative with a reputation for fierceness. His nickname meant spear and referred to an incident thirty years ago in which he had speared a man to death. He had an intense manner; fixing me with his eyes, he said in clipped tones:

"I have only just heard about the black ox today, or else I would have come here earlier. /ontah, do you honestly think you can serve meat like that to people and avoid a fight?" He paused, letting the implications sink in. "I don't mean fight you, /ontah; you are a white man. I mean a fight between Bushmen. There are many fierce ones here, and with such a small quantity of meat to distribute, how can you give everybody a fair share? Someone is sure to accuse another of taking too much or hogging all the choice pieces. Then you will see what happens when some go hungry while others eat."

The possibility of at least a serious argument struck me as all too real. I had witnessed the tension that surrounds the distribution of meat from a kudu or gemsbok kill, and had documented many arguments that sprang up from a real or imagined slight in meat distribution. The owners of a kill may spend up to two hours arranging and rearranging the piles of meat under the gaze of a circle of recipients before handing them out. And I also knew that the Christmas feast at /ai/ai would be bringing together groups that had feuded in the past.

Convinced now of the gravity of the situation, I went in earnest to search for a second cow; but all my inquiries failed to turn one up.

The Christmas feast was evidently going to be a disaster, and the incessant complaints about the meagerness of the ox had already taken the fun out of it for me. Moreover, I was getting bored with the wisecracks, and after losing my temper a few times, I resolved to serve the beast anyway. If the meat fell short, the hell with it. In the Bushmen idiom, I announced to all who would listen:

"I am a poor man and blind. If I have chosen one that is too old and too thin, we will eat it anyway and see if there is enough meat there to quiet the rumbling of our stomachs."

On hearing this speech, Ben!a offered me a rare word of comfort. "It's thin," she said philosophically, "but the bones will make a good soup."

At dawn Christmas morning, instinct told me to turn over the butchering and cooking to a friend and take off with Nancy to spend Christmas alone in the bush. But curiosity kept me from retreating. I wanted to see what such a scrawny ox looked like on butchering, and if there *was* going to be a fight, I wanted to catch every word of it. Anthropologists are incurable that way.

The great beast was driven up to our dancing ground, and a shot in the forehead dropped it in its tracks. Then, freshly cut branches were heaped around the fallen carcass to receive the meat. Ten men volunteered to help with the cutting. I asked /gaugo to make the breast bone cut. This cut, which begins the butchering process for most large game, offers easy access for removal of the viscera. But it also allows the hunter to spot-check the amount of fat on the animal. A fat game animal carries a white layer up to an inch thick on the chest, while in a thin one, the knife will quickly cut to bone. All eyes fixed on his hand as /gaugo, dwarfed by the great carcass, knelt to the breast. The first cut opened a pool of solid white in the black skin. The second and third cut widened and deepened the creamy white. Still no bone. It was pure fat; it must have been two inches thick.

"Hey /gau," I burst out, "that ox is loaded with fat. What's this about the ox being too thin to bother eating? Are you out of your mind?"

"Fat?" /gau shot back, "You call that fat? This wreck is thin, sick, dead!" And he broke out laughing. So did everyone else. They rolled on the ground, paralyzed with laughter. Everybody laughed except me; I was thinking.

I ran back to the tent and burst in just as Nancy was getting up. "Hey, the black ox. It's fat as hell! They were kidding about it being too thin to eat. It was a joke or something. A put-on. Everyone is really delighted with it!"

"Some joke," my wife replied. "It was so funny that you were ready to pack up and leave /ai/ai."

If it had indeed been a joke, it had been an extraordinarily convincing one, and tinged, I thought, with more than a touch of malice as many jokes are. Nevertheless, that it was a joke lifted my spirits considerably, and I returned to the butchering site where the shape of the ox was rapidly disappearing under the axes and knives of the butchers. The atmosphere had become festive. Grinning broadly, their arms covered with blood well past the elbow, men packed chunks of meat into the big cast-iron cooking pots, fifty pounds to the load, and muttered and chuckled all the while about the thinness and worthlessness of the animal and /ontah's poor judgment.

We danced and ate that ox two days and two nights; we cooked and distributed fourteen potfuls of meat and no one went home hungry and no fights broke out.

But the "joke" stayed in my mind. I had a growing feeling that something important had happened in my relationship with the Bushmen and that the clue lay in the meaning of the joke. Several days later, when most of the people had dispersed back to the bush camps, I raised the question with Hakekgose, a Tswana man who had grown up among the !Kung, married a !Kung girl, and who probably knew their culture better than any other non-Bushman.

"With us whites," I began, "Christmas is supposed to be the day of friendship and brotherly love. What I can't figure out is why the Bushmen went to such lengths to criticize and belittle the ox I had bought for the feast. The animal was perfectly good and their jokes and wisecracks practically ruined the holiday for me."

"So it really did bother you," said Hakekgose. "Well, that's the way they always talk. When I take my rifle and go hunting with them, if I miss, they laugh at me for the rest of the day. But even if I hit and bring one down, it's no better. To them, the kill is always too small or too old or too thin; and as we sit down on the kill site to cook and eat the liver, they keep grumbling, even with their mouths full of meat. They say things like, 'Oh this is awful! What a worthless animal! Whatever made me think that this Tswana rascal could hunt!'"

"Is this the way outsiders are treated?" I asked.

"No, it is their custom; they talk that way to each other too. Go and ask them."

/gaugo had been one of the most enthusiastic in making me feel bad about the merit of the Christmas ox. I sought him out first.

"Why did you tell me the black ox was worthless, when you could see that it was loaded with fat and meat?"

"It is our way," he said smiling. "We always like to fool people about that. Say there is a Bushman who has been hunting. He must not come home and announce like a braggard, 'I have killed a big one in the bush!' He must first sit down in silence until I or someone else comes up to his fire and asks, 'What did you see today?' He replies quietly, 'Ah, I'm no good for hunting. I saw nothing at all [pause] just a little tiny one.' Then I smile to myself," /gaugo continued, "because I know he has killed something big.

"In the morning we make up a party of four or five people to cut up and carry the meat back to the camp. When we arrive at the kill we examine it and cry out, 'You mean to say you have dragged us all the way out here in order to make us cart home your pile of bones? Oh, if I had known it was this thin I wouldn't have come.' Another one pipes up, 'People, to think I gave up a nice day in the shade for this. At home we may be hungry but at least we have nice cool water to drink.' If the horns are big, someone says, 'Did you think that somehow you were going to boil down the horns for soup?'

"To all this you must respond in kind. 'I agree,' you say, 'this one is not worth the effort; let's just cook the liver for strength and leave the rest for the hyenas. It is not too late to hunt today and even a duiker or a steenbok would be better than this mess.'

"Then you set to work nevertheless; butcher the animal, carry the meat back to the camp and everyone eats," /gaugo concluded.

Things were beginning to make sense. Next, I went to Tomazo. He corroborated /gaugo's story of the obligatory insults over a kill and added a few details of his own.

"But," I asked, "why insult a man after he has gone to all that trouble to track and kill an animal and when he is going to share the meat with you so that your children will have something to eat?"

"Arrogance," was his cryptic answer.

"Arrogance?"

"Yes, when a young man kills much meat he comes to think of himself as a chief or a big man, and he thinks of the rest of us as his servants or inferiors. We can't accept this. We refuse one who boasts, for someday his pride will make him kill somebody. So we always speak of his meat as worthless. This way we cool his heart and make him gentle."

"But why didn't you tell me this before?" I asked Tomazo with some heat.

"Because you never asked me," said Tomazo, echoing the refrain that has come to haunt every field ethnographer.

The pieces now fell into place. I had known for a long time that in situations of social conflict with Bushmen I held all the cards. I was the only source of tobacco in a thousand square miles, and I was not incapable of cutting an individual off for noncooperation. Though my boycott never lasted longer than a few days, it was an indication of my strength. People resented my presence at the water hole, yet simultaneously dreaded my leaving. In short I was a perfect target for the charge of arrogance and for the Bushmen tactic of enforcing humility.

I had been taught an object lesson by the Bushmen; it had come from an unexpected corner and had hurt me in a vulnerable area. For the big black ox was to be the one totally generous, unstinting act of my year at /ai/ai, and I was quite unprepared for the reaction I received.

As I read it, their message was this: There are no totally generous acts. All "acts" have an element of calculation. One black ox slaughtered at Christmas does not wipe out a year of careful manipulation of gifts given to serve your own ends. After all, to kill an animal and share the meat with people is really no more than Bushmen do for each other every day and with far less fanfare.

In the end, I had to admire how the Bushmen had played out the farce—collectively straight-faced to the end. Curiously, the episode reminded me of the *Good Soldier Schweik* and his marvelous encounters with authority. Like Schweik, the Bushmen had retained a thoroughgoing skepticism of good intentions. Was it this independence of spirit, I wondered, that had kept them culturally viable in the face of generations of contact with more powerful societies, both black and white? The thought that the Bushmen were alive and well in the Kalahari was strangely comforting. Perhaps, armed with that independence and with their superb knowledge of their environment, they might yet survive the future.

Introduction to
*Professionals' Participation in Community
Activities: Is It Part of the Job?*

An anthropologist needs a keen understanding of how the community views itself. He gains this through participant-observation: he maintains a constant awareness of the life of the community while becoming partially integrated into it. The community mental health workers described in this article had to combine the anthropological perspective with their traditional role as passive consultants. Through their direct participation with the parents in the community, they brought about a new understanding of issues that had been previously camouflaged. The initial problem of what was to be taught in the preschool led the parents to take on a re-evaluation of their entire school system, local politics, and police-community relations. Throughout this process the workers refrained from taking on leadership roles themselves, but kept in close enough touch with the community so that they could be called upon to advise the parents and clarify issues.

Redefining the professional role brings with it certain hazards, such as jeopardizing the bureaucracy you represent, and the sense of threat that comes with acknowledging the expertise of local nonprofessional community representatives. The self-confident, flexible professional will not be threatened by the greater understanding of local issues and values that can only come from being a member of the community. The success of this redefinition of the professional role depends upon the professional's constant view of himself as a facilitator, while the community shapes its own goals.

This selection illustrates how community mental health personnel work with perceptions of problems to make them more fully understood. They also help community members to perceive and use their own potential. Through this process community members can find out that their own leadership qualities and effectiveness can bring about the changes they want.

---

4. PROFESSIONALS' PARTICIPATION IN COMMUNITY ACTIVITIES: IS IT PART OF THE JOB?

by Irving N. Berlin, M.D.

With the advent of community mental health centers, it has become much more "professional" for mental health professionals to participate in community activities. For some time now, a number of schools of social work have been teaching courses in community organization and have provided a variety of field-work placements in the community. Courses in social and community psychiatry are increasingly part of the training of psychiatrists, nurses, and psychologists.

It has become clear from the community mental health center movement—especially in or near ghetto areas—that unless mental health professionals become part of their community by participating in some of its activities and by understanding its needs, priorities, and values, the centers may not be of very much use to the community. Where should such training occur, who should do the training, and how should it be done?

Present frameworks taught to mental health professionals provide few guidelines for participating personally, providing models in problem solving through direct involvement, and

From *American Journal of Orthopsychiatry*, Volume 41, No. 3, April 1971, pp. 494–99.

recognizing indications that the community no longer needs one's help in a particular area.

Many mental health workers view their participation in the community and its political activities as something extra-professional, or as a phase in becoming known and trusted in the community. Few, if any, professional schools prepare students for community activities that have political implications. The workers are therefore no more sophisticated in the political process than are the members of the community with whom they work, and they are often less reality based. Although looked to as experts they are in fact usually not expert in the political process. They may learn about the hierarchy of local agency and governmental structure, group processes, and interacting systems, but they rarely know how to go about getting things done, where the leverage is, who can cut the red tape, etc.

Ghetto-area mental health centers and family counseling agencies are often under pressure to become involved in the community's political issues. They are asked to help the community exercise political power to obtain critical health and mental health needs.

In one ghetto community, for example, the schools found themselves in an estranged situation. The community viewed the public schools as an agency that, by default, helped their children fail. Thus, their youngsters would never be educated enough to compete on the open market. The community was angry; they regarded their schools as the Siberia of the total school system: the most ineffective and rigid teachers and administrators were sent there to live out their days. Children with learning problems that required very clear evaluations of their capacities did not receive any special attention. Parents felt their schools could only frustrate them and their children and that effective education was impossible.

The pupil-personnel workers, primarily four social workers, felt it was their function to become involved with the community through several aspects of community participation. First, they attended and participated in Community Council meetings, trying to help the community understand the nature and sources of the pressures faced by the Superintendent and thus learn how he might be influenced. The hope was that the Community Council might more effectively make their needs known and be able to effect change.

Secondly, the mental health professionals, using mental health consultation techniques and consultation with their psychiatric consultant, worked with school personnel to help them become more flexible and attuned to student and community needs. They posed this community's concerns as a unique challenge to evolve a kind of participant and relevant education not yet possible elsewhere in the city. For example, here concerned parents could work as volunteer school aides. They could be trained in a volunteer program and be reliable and effective because they were aware of their children's problems in school.

The third task undertaken by the mental health workers was to become directly involved with parents of disturbed children. Over coffee and doughnuts on a regular open-house basis, they got groups of parents together to discuss their children's problems. Small groups of parents who had children in need of help were involved in activities with groups of children to learn about the helping process, first by observing and later by participating as aides in children's activity groups. In addition, the mental health workers used the part-time school psychologist to evaluate some of these youngsters so teachers were clearly aware of children's needs and of ways they might start helping them.

EFFECTS OF PARTICIPATION IN THE COMMUNITY

The workers viewed their involvement in the community with mixed pleasure in the beginning and then with more professional satisfaction as they saw uninvolved, hostile, or helpless parents become more effective human beings.

One of the most effective, although unplanned, activities was the creation of a preschool program by a private philanthropic organization that hired an experienced and talented preschool teacher and several aides from the community. With parent participation as part of the contract for admission of a child, the school was established for three and four year olds. The organization had one advantage over the Head Start program. It had no connection with an official body, either OEO or the public schools. This meant that its direction *had to be* determined by the teacher, teacher's aides, and parents.

This small program served to augment the inadequately funded Head Start program. While pupil-personnel services had no officially designated role, they functioned in a liaison role to identify children, refer them, and participate with parents and teachers in planning. The need was so great that fathers and mothers were immediately heavily involved in doing the necessary building, painting, and making of equipment. Thus, a feeling of camaraderie and investment developed early. Fathers participated eagerly.

The first crisis faced by the new program centered around a difference of philosophy between the preschool teacher and her aides. The teacher felt that the task of three and four year olds was to play, to learn to verbalize effectively and to become involved in exploratory and creative collaborative play, rather than to learn reading, writing, and numbers. One of the teacher's aides, a black woman who was a very effective disciplinarian, felt that the only way black kids could make it was to learn immediately all the skills necessary for kindergarten and first grade. The other aide, who was of Mexican-American descent, also had some strong question as to whether play itself would really be helpful to the children, although she could involve herself with children effectively in play activities.

The parents very much supported the black aide because they recognized that unless their kids could read, write, and become effective learners very early, they had no chance to make it in school.

At this point the mental health professionals were drawn in. They tended to support the preschool teacher. They pointed out how play can be utilized to develop curiosity and interest in learning and the skills necessary for learning reading and writing. The parents did not buy this concept since they were confronted with a very real problem of recurrent failure of their children in the elementary schools. The question then raised was: should the elementary schools be changed so that they would provide all youngsters with the necessary educational opportunities, or should the preschool be geared to fit in with an outmoded elementary-education methodology?

Parents were now critically concerned with learning more about the total educational process. They asked the teacher and mental health professionals to organize a series of meetings that would help them more effectively assess both the preschool and the primary school educational processes, and to provide them with reading materials.

Discussion at each meeting was active. Parents were deeply involved and sometimes volatile. The speakers found they were required to present their particular points of view with clear facts and illustrations. A number of parents, both mothers and fathers, did their homework very thoroughly, read the material, and presented their interpretations of the articles.

One of the child development experts described with vividness the developmental process from a maturational point of view and how learning occurred at every step. He showed how concept formation develops, how curiosity is stimulated, and how the schools' emphasis on rote learning can interfere with effective concept formation and critical thinking.

At the conclusion, the parents decided the preschool teacher's ideas were correct and their next move had to be to alter the primary schools to which their children were assigned. At this point the mental health professionals indicated that it was more than simply the job of these parents, but rather that of the entire community. The parents agreed to raise the issue at the next Community Council meeting.

A number of stormy meetings followed, in which these parents militantly presented to the Community Council what they expected from the primary schools. Some members of the Council tried to pacify these parents and were reluctant to bring such issues to the attention of the School Board and Superintendent because previous meetings had brought no change.

Since School Board elections were near, however, one member of the Council who had a child in the preschool and one in the elementary school, offered himself as a candidate. The concern of most parents for the education of their children was of such magnitude that they were able to swing the Council into backing their stand and obtained a meeting with the Superintendent and the School Board.

During this meeting, the parents clearly outlined the issues involved in the primary schools and their concern for the education of their children. The President of the School Board and the Superintendent quickly acknowledged the problems and described how overburdened they were with problems throughout the city. It would take time to alleviate the many problems. The Superintendent also called upon some of the mental health professionals who worked for the schools to back up his stand that the elementary school was not "that bad." Caught in the bind between the school that employed them and the community in which they worked, the professionals felt they had to face the issue squarely. Their spokesman was able to define clearly in educational terms why the elementary school's efforts were outmoded and had an adverse impact on the children. The professionals described the kinds of teachers and administrators who had been assigned to these schools and their inflexibility and incapacity to work meaningfully with children, especially those who needed special help. Thus confronted, both the School Board and the Superintendent said they would do what they could to remedy the situation. The parents' group said they would give the Superintendent and the School Board several months to make changes. They said that if the school system failed, their Community Council would find other means of effecting change, such as going directly to the City Council as well as trying to elect a parent to the Board. One of the City Councilmen, as the Board knew, was a resident of this area. His re-election depended very heavily upon his being able to satisfy his constituents.

The mental health workers were later called into the Superintendent's office and asked why they supported the community against the Superintendent. They stated that they had long served this particular community and were familiar with the schools and felt that the requests of the community were both reasonable and justified. As mental health professionals, they had no alternative but to speak the truth. One of them inquired of the Superintendent if he would have preferred she speak untruthfully in order to save the face of the school system. The Superintendent of course replied that he would not want anybody to do this; however, it was clear he was extremely disturbed, and he asked several workers if they had tenure.

THE SNOWBALLING EFFECT

Having become involved with the school and the School Board around the education of their children, the Community Council, led by some of the parents, also became very concerned with the way in which they were being treated by the welfare and health departments. They focused on two problems: First, because there was no welfare agency in their area, they had to go a long way to rectify errors or to make inquiries or complaints. Second, the public health well-baby clinic in their area was inadequately staffed and equipped. Mothers and babies had to wait interminably. The Community Council began to meet with the Director of Public Welfare and with the Director of Public Health.

In this process, parents never previously involved in activities on their own behalf became aware of their potency as they learned the methods and strategies required to gain support from other community members and from individuals in power in the community. They became much more aware of the political process and how they could use it for their own needs. For the first time, the City Councilman who had been elected from this district was asked to help the Community Council with planning. When he did not reply to a letter, he was directed by a delegation to attend to helping them with their strategies, which he did. The progressive state legislator from this area was asked to participate in the Community Council strategy meetings on obtaining more and better school, welfare, and public health services.

During these meetings, the school mental health workers began to describe what data was required in the way of evidence to help support their cause. They encouraged parents to monitor all of the classrooms in the elementary school and to record, hour by hour and day by day, the teaching and learning that was going on. Parents were also encouraged to note in diary form the welfare problems that were occurring, and also the service provided and the number of people who attended the well-baby clinics. They accumulated data on the length of time it took for them to be served and on the number of young mothers who had to walk out unserved. In addition, they gathered information on the number of police harassments of young people that were occurring.

An interesting and now well-known phenomenon began to occur as the preschool parents and the members of the Council began to get a sense of their potential power and effectiveness. Having utilized the mental health professionals to help them discover how they might become effective on their own behalf and having gone through the data gathering process that helped them reach some of their objectives, there next occurred a period of unease and a sense that they no longer needed help from the mental health professionals. This period of strain and uncertainty about the role of the mental health professionals was bridged in two ways. First, it became clear to the parents in the preschool that they still needed expert guidance in the education of their youngsters and help with some of the very disturbed youngsters and their troubled parents. Secondly, in one of the negotiation sessions with the police department, they called upon one of the black mental health professionals to participate. Her very skillful intercession clarified the issues, especially the actual examples of the kind of provocation by the police that resulted in retaliatory behavior by the youth. This led to an experimental period in which some of the officers were relieved of their duties. An effort was made to see what would happen if police officers who had better attitudes toward the youths in the area were provided.

The community leaders realized that improved schools, welfare and public health services were only a beginning, there would be other ways to utilize effectively the professionals' skills.

In another area of the same city a similar undertaking failed. Both the Community Council and concerned parents in this ghetto area, as well as the teachers and mental health professionals, were at constant loggerheads about their mutual objectives. When we examined the issues in this second instance, it became clear that the mental health professionals and educators, though competent professionals, had no expertise or training in helping parents become effective in the community.

Only a new, concerned school administrator was able to help this community organization clarify the issues. His single-minded concern with better education for the students helped mobilize the community to effective action.

PART II
PROBLEMS IN COMMUNITY
INTEGRATION

Those who recognize the positive value of city life emphasize the freedom it allows people to pursue a highly specialized avocational, educational, economic, or occupational goal. But becoming a securities analyst on Wall Street or a coloratura in the Metropolitan Opera means building a new identity different from what a person brings with him. The readings here illustrate how the equipment someone brings with him can be used to smooth the difficult transition into urban life. These identifications can also be used as a basis for revitalization of group membership in an ongoing community.

In the past ten years, identifications based on ascription have become an important part of urban life, and can make it more fulfilling. These new groups, based on sex as in the women's movement, or on color and religion, as with the Black Muslims, or ethnic origin, as with the Italian American Civil Rights League or the Jewish Defense League, constitute a new basis for social action and group membership in urban life. These kinds of groups can play an important part in community integration by giving membership based on a sense of worthiness that has previously gone unrecognized.

Belonging to these groups is the first step toward community integration, for it introduces an associational quality to life. Membership also gives people a sense of personal effectiveness upon forces which often seem to be beyond their control. It is the vested interests of these groups that create strong commitment. The paradox here is that while these groups fulfill members' personal needs, the vested interests can heighten competition with other groups, and threaten to destroy community integration on a larger level.

When any group forms, its ideology in the initial stages will emphasize parochial concerns, such as how its members are discriminated against. Inequities in employment, defamation, and various discriminatory practices become rallying cries for the group. This leads them to attack other groups and see themselves as competing for scarce resources. What emerges is antagonism which can inhibit community integration; the vigilante activities of the Jewish Defense League are a vivid example of how a group can stimulate animosity within a community.

Pressure for assimilation has been important in the United States in contributing to our rejection of differences. Perhaps these movements are necessary to establish more public and official recognition of real differences among people, since ethnic differences have never really disappeared. People appreciate more and more the usefulness of ethnic, racial, and sex differences because they see that these ascribed characteristics can be parlayed into political power.

American society has insisted on a rigid definition of what it means to be an American for immigrant and minority groups. Cities have suppressed differences by imposing arbitrary principles of organization, such as election districts, bureaucratic rules regarding services, and forced urban relocation. In New York City, passing tests in English were until recently requirements for voting and getting a driver's license. Pressure from the Puerto Rican community has brought about the respectability of literacy in Spanish.

The importance of these new groups is that they are self-initiated and thus provide a real sense of membership and effectiveness. The differences that emerge, although they appear to be divisive, could create community integration on a new level in our cities. The democratic process has, in theory at least, welcomed the free expression of conflicts. These groups have the potential for working together through a process of mutual decision-making and political compromise. The challenge of urban life can be best met by the urbanite himself, and he can do it through these voluntary associations.

For this more effective type of community integration to

occur, urban groups must exercise control over what happens in their communities. This means forcing the established political and bureaucratic structures to relinquish their power. This power can then be transferred to community groups through school control, service agencies such as health and public assistance, and consultation regarding urban planning programs. This kind of control is already being exercised, but has had to face strong opposition from more traditional interest groups such as unions. Once power and authority is in the hands of community groups, the decision-making process becomes very different. No longer is public policy initiated from top levels, but rather by the consumers of the services themselves. The process here is one which involves the transition of the groups from dependence to independence, and from submission to responsible control. As group members begin to see themselves differently, they also begin to see the processes that affect them as more complex. As they begin to cope with political realities, they begin to perceive their community as interconnected. The initial demands of community-controlled school boards in New York were for changes in curriculum and the right to hire and fire teachers. Once these demands were met, other more general concerns began to arise, such as safety in the schools and in the neighborhoods. It becomes apparent to community members that all of the institutions that serve a community are dependent on each other, and that the improvement of the community as a whole is essential to any kind of real progress. While this kind of process initially creates animosity toward outsiders and elicits backlash from various segments of the society, it also fosters the strong community feeling necessary for community integration.

Introduction to
The Role of Voluntary Associations in West African Urbanization

The growth of urban centers in developing countries is due to the intense influx of migrants from rural areas. The diverse backgrounds of these migrants has created that heterogeneity which is a fundamental characteristic of the urban condition. It is this diversity that many sociologists feel contributes to chaos, confusion, alienation, and depersonalization in city life. The urban immigrant in a developing country has left behind his traditional, familiar support systems such as his immediate family, his clan and tribe—all of which supply him with the conviction that his way of doing things is right and proper. In the more gradual growth of cities in Western society, membership in such groups could potentially have replaced these traditional supports, but the mutual aid and burial societies have disappeared. Social isolation continues to plague people, and Dial-a-prayer, suicide prevention by telephone, singles bars, and computer dating flourish to combat it.

The migrant to the city from a traditional culture often carries with him a group membership which allows him to re-create feelings of belonging which are not so different from those he has in his village. Kenneth Little explores this group membership in discussing the nature and function of these voluntary associations in West African cities, where the immigrant becomes involved in a wide variety of activities on the basis of his ethnic and tribal identifications.

In a traditional society, group membership is important to a person because he is born into a large system of extended family relationships, lineage and clan ties, tribal membership and groups based on how old he is. This predisposes the migrant fresh from a rich network of ties to seek out group membership in the city, simply because he feels comfortable only when "belonging."

In addition, these memberships meet other needs as well —they provide the migrant with the opportunity to meet a mate on a preferential rather than an arranged basis. He will learn the procedure for getting a job, how to use public transportation, how to use money, how to dress. Through the "club" he will meet already established fellow tribesmen who will informally provide him with contacts for housing and jobs. Above all, membership in this organization provides him with a strong sense of continuity with his traditional background through songs, dances, and rituals.

In the 1930s, Robert Redfield formally theorized that urbanization means secularization, individualization, and disorganization of culture as inescapable and defining elements of city life. This set the tone for social scientists to see cities as Sodoms and Gomorrahs, and this traditional suspicion of city life is still manifest in our political process: rural areas continue to be overrepresented in our state legislatures, and enjoy special Federal subsidies partly because of the value we place on rural way of life. Little shows that the personal quality of primary relationships of rural life in Africa can be brought to and experienced in cities. The nature of the voluntary association, with its emphasis on tradition and coherence, inhibits the rise of individualization, secularization, and disorganization of culture.

This excerpt from Oscar Lewis's study of Puerto Rican family life shows what it is like for a migrant to New York City lacking such supports:

> We left for New York at eleven-thirty in the morning in an Eastern Airlines plane. It was my first airplane trip. Only *mamá*, Cruz and a girl named Hilda came to see us off. Nobody else. The trip took over eight hours because fog delayed us. I was airsick and it seemed to me the flight would never end. I was scared to death and with four children to look after!
>
> . . . Felícita lived in a small one-story house. It wasn't made of wood but of some kind of material they use in New York. It had a living room, a bedroom, bathroom, a small porch and a back yard. It was a very pretty little

house. Fela's husband, Edmundo, was in the hospital. He had had an accident at the graveyard where he worked. Three boarders came to the house to eat and one of them, Lorenzo, also slept there. Sleeping in that house were Felícita, her children Tany and Mundito, Simplicio, Flora, Catín, Sarita, Toya, Quique, myself, *don* Lorenzo and, later, Edmundo. Felícita and Flora slept on the bed and I slept on the floor with all the children. . . .

One of Felícita's boarders was a boy named Eddy. He liked me and I liked him too. We fell in love, but not deeply. Eddy asked me for dates and I went to the movies with him.

One day he and I went to the beach. When we got back Felícita had put Toya's crib outside. I asked her why, and she answered that the crib was in the way. What she meant was that my children and I were in the way. Now she wasn't cooking meals except when she felt like it. Eddy noticed how she treated me and asked me if I would go off with him. That was thirteen days after I had arrived from Puerto Rico. I said yes, not because I loved him but to have a place where I could take my children and live in peace. That boy really did me a favor, taking me out of my sister's house. He found a place in Bridgeboro and we moved there.

I went to work in Bridgeboro picking tomatoes. Eddy worked there too and acted as my interpreter. I had to get up at six o'clock, leave the children with the woman who took care of them, and be on the job by seven. Whichever of us got home first in the evening cooked dinner. I washed our clothes at the *laundry*. Eddy took me there and showed me what coins to use. He never once beat me and we never had a quarrel either. I knew that he liked women but he never told me anything about his life.

There weren't many jobs in Bridgeboro, so after a month we went back to Salem. I got a job packing in a canning factory. Felícita wanted a job too, but they wouldn't hire her because she had worked there before and one day had just walked out. I made ninety to a hundred dollars a week there. *Don* Camacho was sending me about twenty-five dollars every month. I paid twenty-five each week to a lady to take care of my children and twenty dollars a week rent. Felícita had moved out and we were living in her little house.

After a while the lady couldn't come any more to look after the kids, so Felícita took over. One day she didn't

feel like staying with them and just walked off and left
them all alone. The neighbors must have called the cops
because a detective came to get me at the factory. He even
wanted to take me to court. I explained that I had left the
children with my sister, so he let me off. He caught up with
her at the railroad station but didn't do anything to her.
She got mad at me and hardly spoke to me for a while. I
got somebody else for the children but later Felícita took
them back again.

Later, in the Bronx:

My first job was making purses. I worked as an *operator*,
at forty-three dollars a week. . . .

I didn't have a single friend in that place. I don't like
to strike up friendships with the other employees when I
work in a factory. Besides, there's no comradeship among
workers in this country. Most of the Americans would like
to keep all the jobs for themselves, so they won't cooperate
with a Spanish person. I didn't know the work well and I
had to ask how to do things, where to hook on the thread,
and so on. They never had the courtesy to explain. They'd
just say, "I don't know. Ask the boss." Even the Puerto
Rican women were like that. Once I asked a girl named
Feliciana how to turn a purse.

"I'm sorry," she said, "but I can't leave my work to help
you. You have to learn by yourself. The rest of us can't attend you new ones."

I said, "You don't have to make such a big thing of it.
I just asked you a simple question." After that I was never
very friendly with any of them. They were all stuck up.
And I don't take, so I won't have to give, understand? . . .

I have relatives in New York but they were no help at all.
I have many cousins on my father's side who were born in
the States, but they all speak English and we don't keep
up any kind of family relationship. One day I called up
Aunt María del Carmen, whom I had not seen for sixteen
years. I got her telephone number from Uncle Simón. She
said, "Well, if you plan to call on me, come early because
I have to go out." What did that mean? Clearly, that she
didn't want me to come. So I didn't go and I've never
phoned her since. I tore up the slip with her telephone
number. . . .

I had trouble finding a job, so I applied to *welfare*. I

figured that on *relief* I should get about a hundred dollars a month for rent and food. In Puerto Rico, all I got was eighteen dollars. But *welfare* wouldn't accept my case. They said they couldn't help me because I hadn't established residence and because I had no place where I could buy on credit. That's the way they are. . . .

Well, there I was, alone and unable to find work or get on *relief* and already owing rent.*

* Adapted from *La Vida* by Oscar Lewis, Vintage Books, Random House, New York, 1965, pp. 198–206.

---

5. THE ROLE OF VOLUNTARY ASSOCIATIONS IN WEST AFRICAN URBANIZATION

by Kenneth Little

THE URBANIZATION OF WEST AFRICA

. . . What, in effect, this transformation of West Africa involves is a social process somewhat analogous to the social changes that resulted in the urbanization of Western Europe during the nineteenth century. Western contact with Africa, like the Industrial Revolution in Europe, has created new social and psychological needs which life in the countryside is rarely able to satisfy. The consequence is a tremendous migration of men and women to the towns, and to places where money can be earned to pay taxes, to provide bridewealth, and to buy manufactured goods and appliances.

Many of these people are in search of a higher standard of living in the shape of the more up-to-date amenities and better housing as well as the higher income that the town can

Adapted from "The Role of Voluntary Associations in West African Urbanization" by Kenneth Little, *American Anthropologist*, Volume 59, No. 4, August 1957, pp. 579–94.

offer. But this is not the only motivation. A large number of the younger men are looking for further educational opportunities, or are hoping to start a fresh career. Others move as a means of escaping from the restrictions of village life, and some of the younger girls, as well as the boys, out of love of adventure and desire for fresh experiences.

As Fortes has written in reference to the Gold Coast: "Labour, enterprise, and skill are now marketable in their own right anywhere in the country. . . . People feel that there is little risk in moving about, especially if, as appears to be the case with most mobile elements, their earning capacity is low. A clerk getting £2.10 a month feels that he cannot go much lower if he moves." The development of motor transport, in the shape of the ubiquitous lorry, is an important factor in these respects. Not only has it greatly increased local mobility between town and town, and between town and surrounding countryside, but it has created a new and influential social role—that of the lorry-driver, as a go-between between the urban labor market and the rural village.

Most of this migration is in the direction of towns already established as large centers of Western commerce and administration, of the rapidly growing ports, and of places where mining and other industries are being developed. Its effect has been to swell the population of such places far beyond their previous size, as well as to convert a good many villages into urban areas. For example, the principal towns of Senegal in French West Africa increased their populations by 100 per cent between 1942 and 1952 and those of the French Ivory Coast by 109 per cent during the same decade. In the Gold Coast there was an increase of 98 per cent in the populations of the five largest towns between 1931 and 1948. Cotonou in Dahomey grew from 1,100 in 1905 to 35,000 in 1952 and Lunsar, in Sierra Leone, which was a village of 30 inhabitants in 1929, has a population today of nearly 17,000.

Although urbanism in terms of "a relatively large, dense, and permanent settlement of socially heterogeneous individuals" is not a general characteristic of traditional life, it is far from being a unique phenomenon in West Africa. In 1931, some 28 per cent of the Yoruba population of Western Nigeria lived in 9 cities of over 45,000 inhabitants, while a further 34 per cent lived in cities of over 20,000 inhabitants. However, what distinguishes the "new" African city—"new" in the sense, as Georges Balandier points out, that they were built by European colonists—from traditional urbanism is that a large part of its population is industrial, depending upon the labor market for a living. This is particularly evident in the case of towns of recent growth. In Cotonou, for example, some 10,000 persons out of a population of some 35,000 are in wage employment.

A further point is that the modern town is much more heterogeneous. It has groups of professionals, office workers, municipal employees, artisans, etc., and in addition to its indigenous political and social segmentation, it also accommodates a large proportion of "strangers." Not only do the latter frequently outnumber the native inhabitants of the town, but they include a wide diversity of tribes. For example, Kumasi, although the capital of Ashantiland, contains as many non-Ashantis as Ashantis; Takoradi-Sekondi contains representatives of more than sixty different tribes; and less than 10 per cent of the inhabitants of Poto-Poto, one of the three African towns of Brazzaville, were born in that city. In the Gold Coast, as a whole, more than two-thirds of the inhabitants of the big towns have been there for less than five years. A further significant characteristic of these urban populations is the numerical preponderance of young people over old and, to a less appreciable extent, the preponderance of men over women. For example, only 2.4 per cent of the population of Cotonou are over sixty years of age. In 1921, men considerably outnumbered women, but by 1952 the masculinity rate had dropped to 111. In an area of Poto-Poto, on the other hand, where the average age of the population is about twenty-five, there are only 515 females to every 1,000 males.

From the point of view of social organization one of the most striking characteristics of these modern towns is the very large number and variety of voluntary associations. These include a host of new political, religious, recreational, and occupational associations as well as the more traditional mutual aid groups and secret societies out of which some of these more recent organizations have developed. What generally distinguishes the latter kind of association is its more formal constitution and the fact that it has been formed to meet certain needs arising specifically out of the urban environment of its members. It is also more "modern" both in respect to its aims and the methods employed to attain them. One of the best illustrations of these points is provided by certain tribal associations of an extraterritorial kind, known in Nigeria and the Gold Coast as Tribal Unions.

These tribal unions range from little unions, consisting of a few members of the same extended family or clan, to much larger bodies like the Ibo State Union which is a collection of village and clan unions. In Nigeria these associations were originally formed by Ibo and other migrants from Eastern Nigeria to protect themselves from the hostile way in which they were received when they took jobs as policemen, traders, and laborers in the towns of the West and the North. Their aim is to provide members with mutual aid, including support, while out of work, sympathy and financial assistance in the case of illness, and the responsibility for the funeral and the repatriation of the family of the deceased in the case of death. The main raison d'etre however, is that of fostering and keeping alive an interest in tribal song, history, language, and moral beliefs, and thus maintaining a person's attachment to his native town or village and to his lineage there. In furtherance of this sentiment, money is collected for the purpose of improving amenities in the union's home town and to provide its younger people with education. Social activities include the organization of dances on festival days and of sports meetings and games for their young people. Some of these unions also produce an annual magazine, called an Almanac, in which their members' activities are recorded.

Associations based upon membership of the same ethnic group also exist in French and Belgian Africa where they perform somewhat similar functions. In Cotonou, for example, such groups welcome and look after persons newly arrived from the country. They provide a means whereby both the old people and the "evolué" can keep in touch with their rural relatives and friends. Each such association has an annual feast and celebration which brings together everyone from the same region. It is also a means of helping the needy and aged members of the group.

In Nigeria there have also been developed home branches of the tribal union abroad; and as a final step, State unions have been created, comprising every union of members of the same tribe. It is not surprising, therefore, that these Nigerian tribal unions have obtained a power and influence far beyond their original objectives. The larger unions have played an important part in the expansion of education. They offer scholarships for deserving boys and girls and run their own schools. In some places, the monthly contributions of members for education are invested in some form of commercial enterprise, and appeals for money to build schools seem to meet with a particularly ready response. . . .

It was suggested earlier that the social changes resulting from culture contact may be seen as an historical process of adaptation to new conditions. Adaptation in the present context implies not only the modification of African institutions, but their development to meet the demands of an industrial economy and urban way of life. In effect, as Banton has shown in reference to Temne immigrants in Freetown, this sometimes amounts to a virtual resuscitation of the tribal system in the interests of the modernist ambitions and social prestige of the younger educated element concerned. The unpublished findings of Jean Rouch seem to give even greater emphasis to this kind of phenomenon, which he has labelled "super-tribalization." Some of the immigrants into the Gold Coast, whom he has studied, have gained sufficient solidarity through their associations and cults to dominate over the local population, achieving monopolies in various trades. A further important effect of this kind of development is to inhibit the growth of civic loyalty or responsibility for the town concerned. Modern urbanism, in other words, is the conditioning factor in contemporary African society as well as the culmination of so-called acculturation. West African urbanism of course differs from comparable Western situations in being less advanced, although it is probably more dynamic. It involves a particularly rapid diffusion of entirely new ideas, habits, and technical procedures, and a considerable restructuring of social relationships as a consequence of the new technical roles and groups created.

Voluntary associations play their part in both these processes through the fresh criteria of social achievement that they set up and through the scope that they offer, in particular, to women and to the younger age groups. Women, and younger people in general, possess a new status in the urban economy, and this is reflected in the various functions which these associations perform as political pressure groups, in serving as a forum for political expression, and in providing both groups with training in modern methods of business. Equally significant is the fact that women's participation in societies with a mixed membership involves them in a new kind of social relationship with men, including companionship and the opportunity of selecting a spouse for oneself. In particular, voluntary associations provide an outlet for the energies and ambitions of the rising class of young men with a tribal background who have been to school. The individuals concerned are debarred by their "Western" occupations as clerks, school teachers, artisans, etc. and by their youth from playing a prominent part in traditional society proper; but they are the natural leaders of other young people less Westernized and sophisticated than themselves. This is largely because of their ability to interpret the "progressive" ideas they have gained through their work and travel, and through reading newspapers and books, in terms that are meaningful to the illiterate rank and file of the movement.

It is, in fact, in relation to the latter group, particularly the urban immigrant, that the significance of voluntary associations as an adaptive mechanism is most apparent. The newly arrived immigrant from the rural areas has been used to living and working as a member of a compact group of kinsmen and neighbors on a highly personal basis of relationship and mutuality. He knows of no other way of community living than this, and his natural reaction is to make a similar adjustment to urban conditions.

This adjustment the association facilitates by substituting for the extended group of kinsmen a grouping based upon common interest which is capable of serving many of the same needs as the traditional family or lineage. In other words, the migrant's participation in some organization such as a tribal union or a dancing compin not only replaces much of what he has lost in terms of moral assurance in removing from his native village, but offers him companionship and an opportunity of sharing joys as well as sorrows with others in the same position as himself. (Probably an important point in this regard is the large number of offices available in some associations, enabling even the most humble member to feel that he "matters.") Such an association also substitutes for the extended family in providing counsel and protection, in terms of legal aid; and by placing him in the company of women members, it also helps to find him a wife. It also substitutes for some of the economic support available at home by supplying him with sickness and funeral benefits, thereby enabling him to continue his most important kinship obligations. Further, it introduces him to a number of economically useful habits and practices, such as punctuality and thrift, and it aids his social reorientation by inculcating new standards of dress, etiquette, and personal hygiene. Above all, by encouraging him to mix with persons outside his own lineage and sometimes tribe, the voluntary association helps him to adjust to the more cosmopolitan ethos of the city. Equally significant, too, is the syncretistic character of associations of the "traditional-modernized" type. Their combination of modern and traditional traits constitutes a cultural bridge which conveys, metaphorically speaking, the tribal individual from one kind of sociological universe to another.

The latter point is also indicative of various ways in which these voluntary associations substitute for traditional agencies of social control. Not only are positive injunctions to friendly and fraternal conduct embodied in the constitution by which members agree to bind themselves, but many associations have rules proscribing particular misdemeanors and what they regard as antisocial behavior. In this respect, the frequent inclusion of sexual offenses, such as the seduction of the wife or the daughter of a fellow member, is very significant. The association also sets new moral standards and attempts to control the personal conduct of its members in a number of ways. For example, the Lagos branch of *Awo Omama* Patriotic Union resolved not to marry any girl of their town so long as the prevailing amount of money asked for bridewealth was not reduced. The dancing compin will withhold its legal aid from a member unless the company's officials examining the case feel that he is in the right. Also, there are women's groups concerning themselves specifically with the settlement of domestic quarrels, which expel members who are constant troublemakers in the home and among other women. More frequently, punishment takes the form of a fine, but the strongest sanction probably lies in the fact that every reputable association is at pains to check fresh applications for membership. In other words, a person who has earned a bad name for himself in one organization may find it difficult to get into another; and this form of ostracism may in some cases be as painful as exile from the tribe.

A final important point is the extent to which disputes of a private or domestic nature, which would formerly have been heard by some traditional authority such as the head of a lineage, are now frequently taken to the head of an association, even when the matter is quite unconcerned with the life of that particular body.

Introduction to
Second Generation Migrants in Ghana and the Ivory Coast

While Little dealt with people who came to the city with strong tribal affiliations, Rouch deals with the problems of second generation migrants who have lost their traditional culture. The special kind of migration Rouch describes led to the breakdown of important ethnic and tribal ties. The second generation children, stigmatized by the absence of traditional status, managed to compensate by developing organizations that provide them with a common social life and the chance to meet eligible partners, domestic grants to newly married couples, and mutual aid benefits that substitute for traditional support from an extended family or lineage.

We can compare this unique kind of group to groups of people in our own culture who through mental illness or homosexuality are cut off from or stigmatized by family and community. The current rise in gay liberation movements which provide dating and counseling services, a basis for political action, and above all a chance for affiliation illustrates the urban potential for the person who is seen as deviant by the larger society.

The capacity to form these groups again shows us the human potential for meeting important human needs in the urban setting. In fact, the anonymity often considered a negative feature of city life might be considered an advantage here. Only in the large city with its wide variety of activities can people with varied and often unique interests find each other.

6. SECOND GENERATION MIGRANTS IN GHANA AND THE IVORY COAST

by Jean Rouch

Migrants come from West African savannah territories: Upper Volta, Sudan, Niger, northern Ivory Coast, Ghana, Togo, Dahomey, and Nigeria. They leave their homelands to go to the coastal area of the Gulf of Guinea, mainly the forest zone of the Ivory Coast and Ghana. Most are young men temporarily engaged in various occupations and trying to return to their own territories every year. The movement is encouraged by the fact that the season for the cocoa crop corresponds to the dry season in the northern territories. The young men are therefore able to go south between October and March to work on the cocoa farms when they would otherwise be unoccupied at home, and in the cocoa off-season they can return north for the rains when farm work is heaviest. A certain number of wealthy migrants settle temporarily in the south, but even after years without going back they preserve very close links with their original group. On a rough estimation there are from 2,000 to 3,000 migrants in Ghana and 150,000 to 300,000 in Ivory Coast during the season.

From the historical point of view these movements to the coast are the answer to a very old wish of the Sudanese empires to reach the sea. The landing of Europeans about the sixteenth century on the West African coast reversed the direction of the great trade routes. Empires, which until then had their main commercial links with Europe and the Near East across the Sahara, started trading with the south. Important exchange markets developed on the edge of the forest

From *Social Change in Modern Africa*, edited by Aidan Southall, Oxford University Press (International African Institute), London, 1961, pp. 300–4.

at Kong, Bondouke, Kintampa, Salaza, Zugu, and later Kumasi. Cattle and slaves were exchanged for clothes and European goods. The famous nineteenth-century raiders, the Sudanese Samori and the Nigerian Babaku, trying to extend their influence further southward, attracted a lot of young and determined men to the middle part of the Ghana and Ivory Coasts. After the establishment of European settlements the military movement changed into migration in search of a job and the adventures of the long journey to the south became substitutes for the old military saga. From the middle of last century it has become accepted in the savannah that to be a real man you have to have been to the Coast at least once.

From the ethnic point of view the migrations involve mainly Upper Volta tribes. In rural parts of Ghana and Ivory Coast the Moshi are the most important group. They are mainly employed in manual work and play an important part in local farming. The Sudanese in the Ivory Coast started as labourers on European plantations, buying their own land after about five years. They are now traders and farmers, whereas the Nigerian migrants are exclusively traders, mainly dealing in cloth both in urban and rural areas.

These migrations have a considerable influence on the economy of both countries of origin and destination. In Ghana it seems that 60 per cent of the labourers are from the northern territories of Ghana and Upper Volta. In the Ivory Coast 90 per cent of plantation labourers are from Upper Volta. The territories of origin receive a very important contribution to their revenue. In the western districts of the Niger territories 80 per cent of income tax is paid out of money sent back from Ghana and Ivory Coast by the migrants. Obviously there are also political implications.

The majority of migrants are single, either in the sense of being unmarried or of having left their wives and children in rural areas. Very few women migrate from the north, although by contrast coastal migrations appear to attract more women than men, as in the case of Yoruba and Calabar. The result is that many relationships spring up between northern men and coastal women. The unskilled and the poor most frequently cohabit with professional prostitutes whose fees are low and uniform. Amongst returning migrants and those with more stable incomes longer-term relationships are established with indigenous women. A young Gao man employed by an Ashanti mammy may become her boy friend after a time. Or a young Divule from Treichville may ask a Baoule mammy to lend him her daughter during his stay.

Finally, amongst the more settled migrants, marriages with women found in the city are relatively frequent. There are many cases of migrants with wives and children in both northern and coastal areas. In fact, the migrant does not try to marry a woman of his own or a neighbouring group. Northern migrants seem to favour certain indigenous groups of women. That is why in the whole Ivory Coast Baoule women enjoy a particularly high reputation and become the preferred wives of migrants. Children born from such unions find themselves divided between the two kin groups.

If the woman comes from a matrilineal and the man from a patrilineal society their child belongs by custom to both groups. The conflict emerges at marriage according to the customs then followed. Young migrants tend to adopt the customs of the coast, because they are more flexible than those of the north. Verbal agreement followed by the making of a small gift is sufficient to give a union legal sanction, but it is regarded as a state of concubinage or temporary cohabitation rather than marriage, and is damaging to the prestige of the older migrants with more secure incomes. They therefore attempt to marry women according to their own Islamic customs, which include dowry payment and expensive ceremonies. Acceptance of Islam by the wife is also necessary. However, women know that acceptance of Islamic marriage involves the loss of all claim to the children by them in case of separation, so they frequently hesitate to marry or insist on very high dowries.

Even among settled migrants such inter-tribal marriages do not usually last long. The more frequent causes of separation are the husband's return to his country, or the constant interference of the wife's family in domestic affairs. Whatever the system of marriage followed, both parents attempt from the start to take the children. In the case of most migrants interviewed in Ghana and the Ivory Coast, it was apparent that

hey wished to send their children to their own villages as
oon as they were weaned, on the pretext that coastal condi-
ions are not good for children. This is a precaution by the
father, more or less frustrated, to prevent his wife from taking
their children. In the father's village the child will be brought
up as a member of the patrilineage. He will be initiated and
eventually receive the tribal markings. Should he return to
the coast he will always be a member of his patrilineage.

With the slightest excuse, such as illness, mothers try to
send their children to their own family. When migration first
started, husbands allowed themselves to be caught out in this
way and there were many complaints from them about lost
children. The most striking example of this kind is to be
found among the Kotokoli women of Middle Togoland, who
come to South Ghana for the express purpose of prostitution
in order to have children and, of course, the money. Most
of them are married women, but nevertheless many marry
young northern migrants, who are considered to be the most
handsome men. As soon as the children are of an age at which
they may travel, they run away with them. If the father pur-
sues them he often arrives only to find his children with Kotokoli tribal markings, belonging to the family of their Kotokoli
mother.

Most frequently the children who are torn between their
parents in this way settle on the coast, casually brought up
by the mother and educated by the father at minimum expense. They are called *dankasa* meaning "born in foreign
lands." In both Ghana and the Ivory Coast they form a distinct mixed group held apart by both the indigenous coastal
people and the migrants. Belonging to neither the maternal
nor the paternal group they have no tradition and attempt
to create customs of their own. This marginal category is considered by all informants to be unintelligent, unambitious,
and lazy. Migrants attempt to eliminate them and coast people discourage their scholarly pursuits.

Those who have reached adulthood form a sort of inter-
mediary class concerning itself with petty trading and semiskilled occupations, bad taxi-drivers, non-specialized fitters,
semi-literate clerks, and shop assistants.

Rejected by all, they have formed themselves into separate

groups, finding compensation in creating voluntary societies where loneliness, despair, and dreams are shared. This has led to the creation of *goumbe* societies in the Ivory Coast. Initially similar to the many mutual societies found on the coast, the *goumbes* rapidly become young people's dance societies. There are membership fees and general meetings which elect numerous office-bearers; they meet every Sunday to dance and to elect the best couple. But the *goumbes* go even further; more recently they have replaced the maternal and paternal kin groups. Young *goumbe* boys and girls intermarry by preference and the marriage ritual has little similarity with the parents' customs. For example, one frequently finds free unions preceding marriage; and the traditional dowry has been replaced by a "domestic grant" ("subvention du ménage") given by the *goumbe* to enable the couple to buy necessities such as furniture, kitchen equipment, etc. This suggests the development of a new type of community; a community of the rejected, but of people who have withstood contempt and are creating a new way of life.

Introduction to
The American Indian and Federal Policy

Just as Rouch's second-generation migrants have invented a group identity where none existed, the American Indian is in the process of reformulating the concept of Indian-ness to be more useful in the urban setting. Feelings of being an Indian not only come from within, but are a direct result of being categorized as Indians by others. This takes on an even greater significance in the light of the heterogeneity of the urban setting, and becomes a basis for the Indian to translate his identity into political pressure.

It is an interesting paradox of a pluralistic society that historically disenfranchised people can translate their powerlessness into power by using their group membership as a means for action. Public policy administered through the Bureau of Indian Affairs has historically forced the Indian into a position of paternalistic dependency. The Indians have now seized the initiative in defining for themselves the services they require. In so doing, the urban Indian is developing interpersonal skills that will allow him to control and direct the course of his own life. Becoming an active political participant by investigating, demonstrating, and bargaining is an important step in adapting to city life.

The range of services available to the urban Indian is different from the nature and quality of the services the Bureau of Indian Affairs and the Indian Health Service provide on the reservation. Suddenly the Indian migrant finds he must qualify for services on the basis of where he lives, how long he has lived there, and how much money he makes rather than being offered these services solely on the basis of being an Indian. It is this inconsistency which makes him aware of the value of his ethnic identity and makes him wish to exploit it. What emerges is a political pressure group prepared to deal with arbitrary policies which they feel discriminate against urban Indians. The aspect of the Pan-Indian movement is an effort to reinterpret a dependent, restricted position so that it allows him to reap the benefits of the variety and opportunities of the city without losing the traditional services of the Bureau of Indian Affairs.

The same process occurs among other recipients of public services. Public Assistance client activism is one of the most profound changes in how the client perceives the agency. Traditionally the client has no voice in either the formulation of policy or the procedural aspects of the services he receives. It is only recently that the client has taken the initiative in deciding what he wants and how he wants it. Like the American Indian, he is acquiring new skills and an autonomous redefinition of himself which gives him real political power. Other groups such as Senior Citizens, returning veterans, and consumer groups illustrate this transition from dependency to autonomy.

Suddenly we find in our cities the emergence of grass roots pressure groups forming around immediate needs. This is happening because there is a gap between the way the government sees peoples' needs and the way the people see them. This potential for social change based on common concerns could only exist in the city because only there can enough people be found who are touched by some issues. As they become more skilled in dealing with the diverse urban environment, it will become increasingly important for the service agency to respond to its clients as people who have achieved control over their own lives.

7. THE AMERICAN INDIAN AND FEDERAL POLICY

by James E. Officer

Indians within a reservation setting enjoy a closer relationship with the federal government than do most other Americans. While federal taxes help to finance many programs of benefit to citizens generally, few of these are actually *administered by* federal agencies. Instead, federal funds in the form of grants or loans find their way into the hands of *local* administrators. On Indian reservations, however, federal officials actually build and run schools, operate vocational training programs, provide scholarships to Indian students, supply medical care and hospital services, help individuals to find jobs, appraise lands, arrange leases, administer sales of minerals and timber, collect rentals, distribute checks to landowners, and supply general welfare assistance directly to Indian clients.

Not only are programs for reservation Indians administered at a different level of government from those for other Americans, but the quality of the programs is often different. Outside the military departments, only the Indian Health Service supplies its clients with cradle-to-grave medical and hospitalization services; no other agency at any level of government provides a program for training individuals and helping them to find employment which is as comprehensive as the employment assistance effort of the Indian Bureau; few local welfare agencies administer programs of general welfare assistance with the same flexibility as the Indian Bureau; and no other

Adapted from "The American Indian and Federal Policy" by James E. Officer in *The American Indian in Urban Society*, edited by Jack O. Waddell and D. Michael Watson, Little, Brown and Company, Boston, 1971, pp. 55–63.

PROBLEMS IN COMMUNITY INTEGRATION

agency of government has a program of higher education grants like that maintained by the BIA.

When an Indian leaves the reservation and settles in the city, he does not lose his eligibility for the services which grow out of the federal trusteeship over Indian reservation land. If he has an interest in an allotment, he may benefit from services related to appraising the value of his allotment and the resources it contains, negotiating leases and sales, collecting rentals, royalties and sale receipts, and distributing income—all of which the BIA supplies to holders of trust allotments wherever they may be living.

It is the so-called "community" services—rather than those related to federal trusteeship—which do not usually follow Indians to the cities. Even in the case of persons relocated under Indian Bureau auspices, eligibility for such services is terminated in a short time. Within the BIA, the rationalization for withholding community services from Indians living away from the reservation has been that such individuals pay taxes in their communities and, therefore, should be served by the local agencies, which these taxes support, rather than by the Indian Bureau. Reservation Indians, on the other hand, contribute few tax revenues to local agencies and are often not subject to their jurisdiction. Therefore, special federal services are required for them.

The explanation in the case of the Indian Health Service is somewhat different. In the basic legislation establishing the agency and in subsequent appropriations acts, Congress has indicated that it intends reservation Indians to be the principal clientele served. Only in one instance (a clinic in Rapid City, South Dakota, operated for the benefit of Indians residing there) has it departed from this position.

The Indian who has recently migrated to the city from a reservation home encounters three new elements in his quest for assistance from public agencies. First, there is no agency which serves only Indian clients; he must stand in the same line with others in applying for and receiving such services. Second, he is usually eligible for help only if he is indigent. And, third, the character of services provided by state welfare institutions and public hospitals is different from that provided by the U. S. Public Health Service and other federal agencies whose services are geared primarily to the local Indian clientele in the Indian setting.

In an earlier day, many off-reservation Indians were persons who had voluntarily surrendered tribal status in order to enjoy full citizenship rights and the greater economic security which they felt could be found outside the reservations. These persons seldom expected or asked for special consideration. Other off-reservation Indians had no tribal affiliations or belonged to landless tribes. Many of these persons had never benefitted from special federal attention and were not sufficiently familiar with the reservation situation to know what services federal agencies were providing there.

Following the allotment program and the establishment of off-reservation boarding schools, a new class of Indians began to settle in the cities. These were "tribal" Indians—persons from reservation communities—some of whom, while not always satisfied with the services provided "back home" by the Indian Bureau, expected that agency to support them and come to their rescue in time of trouble in their new surroundings. By the twenties, when the Meriam report was prepared, the cities contained a sufficient number of these persons to be concerned about their impact, especially upon the welfare agencies. These Indians were also important enough as a class by this time to merit a lengthy chapter in the report.

Meriam and his associates observed that the feeling among migrated Indians toward the Indian Bureau was much more bitter than among those on the reservations. They attributed this bitterness to the following factors: many of the migrants had left the reservations because of difficulties with federal officials and objection to federal policies; as a group they were probably more "resourceful, energetic, and better educated" than other Indians; they were not so fearful of what might result from outspoken criticism of the BIA; and, finally, they had had "more opportunity to contrast what the government does for the Indians with what the ordinary city does for its citizens."

As a former official of the Indian Bureau, I can contrast the last conclusion of the Meriam survey with the one which I derived from many conversations with urban Indians during the 1960s. These Indians were much more displeased with the BIA because of its failure to provide them the same range of services provided their reservation kinsmen than because of the fact that the "ordinary city" does more for its citizens than does "the government for the Indians," as is suggested by the authors of the Meriam report. It may well be that the federal government in the last forty years has come closer to meeting the needs of Indian citizens than local governments have to meeting the needs of their constituencies.

Urban Indians today are no less bitter toward the Bureau of Indian Affairs and the Indian Health Service than were their counterparts forty years ago. Much of the leadership for the more militant Indian movements today has come from Indians who reside away from the reservations. That some of their bitterness relates to the question of eligibility for special federal services is documented in the words of the executive director of a new national organization composed of urban Indians. Formed in 1968 and initially funded with a $90,000 grant from the Ford Foundation, the group is known as American Indians United. In 1969, its executive director was quoted as saying that the purpose of the organization is "to strengthen the urban Indian's identity" and "to obtain for him both from private and Federal sources, the same services that are now provided for the reservation Indians."

The 1960 census reported 165,922 "urban" Indians in the United States, which was about 30 per cent of the total Indian population. . . .

There can be little doubt that urbanization of Indians has continued during the 1960s and—at least in terms of actual numbers—has accelerated. The BIA employment assistance program has been the factor of greatest importance in stimulating increases in the urban Indian population. During the 1950s, the Indian Bureau assisted nearly 30,000 Indians to relocate to urban areas, and provided vocational training leading to off-reservation employment for about 1,600 family heads, who together with their dependents numbered around 3,500 persons. Between 1960 and 1968, these figures—especially the numbers of individuals enrolled in vocational training programs—were substantially increased. Nearly 38,000 persons were helped to settle in cities, and vocational training was provided about 20,000 family heads, who with their dependents totaled slightly over 32,500 individuals (BIA 1968). In its 1970 budget requests, the BIA outlined a five-year program which would enable 58,000 additional Indians to take advantage of employment opportunities in urban areas by the end of 1974. . . .

What is the significance of the movement of Indians into the cities? Enough has transpired to provide some basis for prediction. From the point of view of individual tribes, the strongest impacts may come at the reservation level, for example, increasing demands from urban Indians that they be better represented on tribal councils. It is already evident that the nonresident members of many tribes have no faith in the desire or ability of present tribal leaders to protect their interest in the tribal estate. Young, aggressive, citified Indians often regard such persons as "Uncle Tomahawks" who are unnecessarily submissive to BIA and other federal officials. Council members who advocate investing income from successful claims suits in long-range reservation development programs are often outvoted by factions led by absentee members who prefer per capita payments. On such reservations as the Spokane, Colville, Flathead, and Blackfeet, the 1960s saw many bitter quarrels between factions composed of resident and nonresident members. In the Colville case, the off-reservation faction even went so far as to advocate liquidation of the entire tribal estate and distribution of the income resulting therefrom.

Another consequence of the urban movement manifest at the reservation level is the so-called "brain drain" of younger, better educated members upon whom the tribes must depend for future leadership. The outmigration of the past twenty years has included primarily individuals under thirty-five years of age. The industrial development program of the Indian Bureau—faced with numerous obstacles, including underfinancing and the isolation of many reservations in terms of transportation and communication—has enjoyed quite limited success, and employment opportunities remain inadequate to attract younger members back to their home communities.

The reservations will also be affected by the fact that, while preserving their interest in receiving benefits from the tribal estate, urban Indians over time will find their tribal ties attenuating, although they may retain a sense of Indian identity and participate in such pan-Indian movements as American Indians United. The whole topic of pan-Indianism is of great importance in discussing the migration of Indians to the cities. In concluding his report based on research among the Indians of Los Angeles, Price noted that:

> An awakened pan-Indianism . . . often becomes an additional dimension to, and sometimes a substitute for . . . tribal affiliations. Although only one-fifth of our respondents are socially active in pan-Indian associations, the great majority of Indians in the city clearly are ideologically and emotionally affiliated with pan-Indianism. Pan-Indianism thus seems to emerge as a stabilizing element—and perhaps a permanent part—of the adaptation of the Indian migrant to the metropolitan areas, and a significant facet of the ethnic diversity of the American city (Price 1968: 175).

The impact of increased Indian urbanization could well be felt by federal agencies, too, including those with special Indian programs. Whether or not American Indians United will succeed in its campaign to extend to urban Indians all the community services which the federal government now provides those who reside on the reservations, there are some indications that the Indian Bureau and the Indian Health Service are modifying their traditional positions to some degree. Examples include the establishment with Congressional blessing of an Indian Health Clinic in Rapid City, South Dakota, and a decision by the BIA in 1969 to experiment with the extension of its housing improvement program (HIP) to some of the urban Indian families. Previously, the HIP program has benefitted only reservation families who could not obtain improved housing by any other means. For several years, the Indian Health Service has provided medical and hospital care for indigent Indians recently moved to the cities until they satisfy the residence requirements for assistance from local health agencies. Since the early 1960s, the Indian Bureau has also followed a policy (which it has never publicized) of providing certain services to Indians in the cities when the failure to receive such services would force them to return to the reservations (where they would again become eligible). However, relatively few individuals—and primarily only those in cities near the reservations—have benefitted from this policy. (The bureau does not maintain separate records for Indians in this category.)

Should the Indian Bureau and the Indian Health Service undertake on a broad scale to provide services to urban Indians, problems would unquestionably arise regarding the overlapping jurisdiction of federal and local public agencies. Historically, local agencies, especially with respect to social welfare and medical care benefits, have often resisted assuming responsibility for local Indians, while the Indian Bureau has fought—sometimes through lawsuits—to establish clearly the principle that Indians away from the reservations are entitled to the same public services from the same agencies available to other Americans in similar circumstances. A reversal of federal policy now would introduce a large measure of confusion into this situation and doubtless prompt some communities to withhold assistance from Indians they now serve.

On the other hand, as long as reservation kinsmen of the urban Indians receive desired special services denied the latter, as long as significant differences remain between the services (such as housing, medical care, and employment assistance) provided reservation Indians by the federal government and those provided the urban citizens, and as long as some local government agencies continue to regard Indians as a peculiar federal responsibility and attempt to deny them services, the issue of whether the "Great White Father" shall follow the Indian to the city will continue to evoke lively controversy.

Introduction to
Life in the West End

We now turn to an urban community in Boston which contained a pre-existing integrative social system which urban planners failed to recognize, and destroyed in the process of redevelopment. Many formal organizations, grass roots neighborhood and block associations are working toward creating a sense of community in low rent districts such as Bedford-Stuyvesant and Harlem. Since it already exists in some form in every community, it is vital to recognize and use it as a foundation for further action. Such a simple procedure as seeing how a person spends his day within the neighborhood, or observing the use of public space such as sidewalks and stoops, helps one realize what makes the people of a community feel connected to it.

Since the quality of group life in the West End was primarily informal, the relocation process was devastating since it was the very physical proximity that contributed to the West Enders' social integration. As Gans points out the West Enders were not consulted about "their" urban renewal and relocation program. It was arbitrarily imposed upon them by a municipal government seeking higher tax yields from a downtown area. Even though they felt that relocation would mean the loss of their irreplaceable way of life, the nature of the informal "peer group" could neither contend with the politics of fighting relocation nor mobilize into a formal association challenging the proposal. Perhaps organization based on geographical proximity, while as valuable as any other, is more fragile than groups based on formal membership.

8. LIFE IN THE WEST END

by Herbert J. Gans

As a neighborhood is more than an ecological or statistical construct, some of its qualities can perhaps be captured only on paper by the sociologically inclined poet or artist. Typical aspects of West End life and the "feel" of the area can best be described by an informal sketch of what so often struck me as an urban village.

To begin with, the concept of the West End as a single neighborhood was foreign to the West Enders themselves. Although the area had long been known as the West End, the residents themselves divided it up into many subareas, depending in part on the ethnic group which predominated, and in part on the extent to which the tenants in one set of streets had reason or opportunity to use another. For example, the social distance between the upper and the lower end was many times its geographical distance.

Until the coming of redevelopment, only outsiders were likely to think of the West End as a single neighborhood. After the redevelopment was announced, the residents were drawn together by the common danger, but, even so, the West End never became a cohesive neighborhood.

My first visit to the West End left me with the impression that I was in Europe. Its high buildings set on narrow, irregularly curving streets, its Italian and Jewish restaurants and food stores, and the variety of people who crowded the streets when the weather was good—all gave the area a foreign and exotic flavor. At the same time, I also noticed the many vacant shops, the vacant and therefore dilapidated tenements, the cellars and alleys strewn with garbage, and the desolation

From *The Urban Villagers* by Herbert J. Gans, The Free Press, New York, 1962, pp. 11–16.

on a few streets that were all but deserted. Looking at the area as a tourist, I noted the highly visible and divergent characteristics that set it off from others with which I was familiar. And, while the exotic quality of the West End did excite me, the dilapidation and garbage were depressing, and made me a little fearful of doing a participant-observation study.

After a few weeks of living in the West End, my observations—and my perception of the area—changed drastically. The search for an apartment quickly indicated that the individual units were usually in much better condition than the outside or the hallways of the buildings. Subsequently, in wandering through the West End, and in using it as a resident, I developed a kind of selective perception, in which my eye focused only on those parts of the area that were actually being used by people. Vacant buildings and boarded-up stores were no longer so visible, and the totally deserted alleys or streets were outside the set of paths normally traversed, either by myself or by the West Enders. The dirt and spilled-over garbage remained, but, since they were concentrated in street gutters and empty lots, they were not really harmful to anyone and thus were not as noticeable as during my initial observations.

Since much of the area's life took place on the street, faces became familiar very quickly. I met my neighbors on the stairs and in front of my building. And, once a shopping pattern had developed, I saw the same storekeepers frequently, as well as the area's "characters" who wandered through the streets every day on a fairly regular route and schedule. In short, the exotic quality of the stores and the residents also wore off as I became used to seeing them.

The attractions that the West End had for the people who had lived there for a long time became evident quickly. Apartments were extremely cheap. I paid only $46 for a six-room apartment with central heating. Long-time residents paid as little as $35 for one like it, and $15 to $25 for a similar unit without central heating. The rooms were large and the apartments comfortable. In buildings without central heating, the apartments were heated with the large combination cooking and heating stoves placed in the kitchen.

At first, I thought that the buildings without central heat-

ing were slums, but I soon learned otherwise. The kitchen
stoves freed the West Enders from dependence on the landlords and their often miserly thermostats. Moreover, people
with stoves could heat their apartments to their own specifications, making them as warm as they liked. In a cold spell,
the kitchen stoves were less desirable, for the rooms furthest
away from the kitchen were cool, and, when the temperature
went down to 10 degrees above zero, the outside bedroom
was icy. Some people placed smaller oil or kerosene stoves
in these rooms, and these occasionally caused fires, although
the kitchen stove was completely safe. Needless to say, central
heating was cheaper in the long run, for people had to buy
oil to heat the stove. Usually, the oil was purchased in quantity, and stored in the cellar. Poorer people had to buy it
in smaller amounts. The apartments also were equipped with
gas water-heaters, which required West End families to heat
their own water, but also assured independence from landlord
whims.

The apartments did, of course, have a number of faults.
The buildings were old and not easy to keep clean. Windows
leaked and the plumbing had its quirks. There were rats in
many of the cellars—although they rarely disturbed anyone except the janitor. No one liked these faults and almost everybody wanted a modern apartment that lacked these disadvantages. However, people were happy with the low rents they
were charged in the West End; modernity is not much of
an advantage when it depletes the family budget.

Of course there were people, especially the very poorest,
who lived in badly substandard housing where the toilets were
shared or broken, the rats were a danger, the oil stove did
not heat properly, and the leaks in the windows could not
be sealed. Such people, who were probably also paying higher
rents, suffered from all the ills of poor housing. When it
comes to livability standards, there is little difference between
the classes. Although poorer people do not have as high expectations as the well-to-do, they are no more willing to live
with defective plumbing than anyone else.

Everyday life in the West End was not much different
from that in other neighborhoods, urban or suburban. The
men went to work in the morning, and, for most of the day,

the area was occupied largely by women and children—just as in the suburbs. There were some men on the street: the older, retired ones, as well as the young and middle-aged ones who either were unemployed, worked on night shifts, or made their living as gamblers. In the afternoon, younger women could be seen pushing baby carriages. Children of all ages played on the street, and teenagers would "hang" on the corner, or play ball in the school yard. The West End's lone playground was fairly dilapidated, and usually deserted. Many women went shopping every day, partly to meet neighbors and to catch up on area news in the small grocery stores, and partly to buy foods that could not be obtained in the weekly excursion to the supermarket. On Sunday mornings, the streets were filled with people who were visiting with neighbors and friends before and after church.

The average West End resident had a choice between anonymity and total immersion in sociability. A few people had moved into the area to hide from the world, and, while visible to their neighbors, could discourage contact, and thus feel anonymous. Generally speaking, however, neighbors were friendly and quick to say hello to each other, although more intense social contact was limited to relatives and friends. Deviant behavior, as displayed by the area "characters," the bohemians, or the middle-class residents was, of course, highly visible. As long as the West Enders were not affected personally, however, they were tolerant. Yet this tolerance was ambivalent: people objected to deviants grudgingly but explained that such kinds of people must be expected in a low-rent neighborhood. At the same time, they found deviant behavior a lively and readily available topic of conversation, which not only provided spice and variety for gossip, but also an opportunity to restate and reaffirm their own values. The bohemians and the schizophrenic characters also served as sources of community amusement, although the latter usually received friendly greetings from other West Enders, even if they did laugh at them once their backs were turned. On the whole, however, the various ethnic groups, the bohemians, transients, and others could live together side by side without much difficulty, since each was responsive to totally different reference groups. Also, at various points, the diverse cultures had common values. For example, everyone liked the low rents, the cheapness of the cost of living generally, and the convenience to downtown. Moreover, as Italians like to stay up late, and to socialize at high decibel levels, the bohemians' loud parties were no problem, at least to them.

The sharing of values was also encouraged by the residential stability of much of the population. Many West Enders had known each other for years, if only as acquaintances who greeted each other on the street. Everyone might not know everyone else; but, as they did know something about everyone, the net effect was the same, especially within each ethnic group. Between groups, common residence and sharing of facilities—as well as the constant struggle against absentee landlords—created enough solidarity to maintain a friendly spirit. Moreover, for many families, problems were never far away. Illnesses, job layoffs, and school or discipline problems among the children occurred regularly. Alcoholism, mental illness, desertion, the death of a loved one, serious financial difficulties, and even violence were familiar to everyone. If they did not take place in one's immediate family, they had happened at some time to a relative or a neighbor. Thus when emergencies occurred, neighbors helped each other readily; other problems were solved within each ethnic group.

For most West Enders, then, life in the area resembled that found in the village or small town, and even in the suburb. Indeed, if differences of age and economic level among the residents were eliminated, many similarities between the life of the urban neighborhood and the suburb would become visible.

Age and class differences are, of course, crucial; they, rather than place of residence, shape the lives of people. That West Enders lived in five-story tenements and suburbanites occupy single-family houses made some—but not many—differences in their ways of life and the everyday routine. For example, although the West Enders were less than a mile from the downtown department stores, it is doubtful whether they used these more than the average suburbanite who has to travel forty-five minutes to get to them. Not all city neighborhoods are urban villages, of course, and there are few similarities among the urban jungle, the apartment hotel district, and the suburb, or for that matter, the urban village.

Although it is fashionable these days to romanticize the slum, this has not been my purpose here. The West End was not a charming neighborhood of "noble peasants" living in an exotic fashion, resisting the mass-produced homogeneity of American culture and overflowing with a cohesive sense of community. It was a run-down area of people struggling with the problems of low income, poor education, and related difficulties. Even so, it was by and large a good place to live.

Introduction to
The Ras Tafari Movement in Jamaica:
A Study of Race and Class Conflict

People who have suffered deprivation often turn to fantasy. Ras Tafari as an organization has as its aim the political, economic, and social autonomy for its members, and social change. Where it differs from other community-based movements is in the highly magical means it employs to achieve these goals. While the wished-for goals are sweeping and revolutionary, the means of achieving them are felt to be out of the hands of the members and under the control of remote figures that have no realistic connection to the organization: i.e., Haile Selassie. As long as the use of magical thinking pervades the movement, it reinforces omnipotent fantasies and makes the movement real only to its members.

Urbanization throws people in close proximity, making them aware of painful differences in opportunities and advantages. Making sense of the world is a basic human need, and if the inconsistencies in economic status are so great that they cannot be dealt with or reconciled in a rational way, people look to magical formulas. Members of Ras Tafari live on the margins of political and economic life in Jamaica, but this in no way excludes the possibility of its developing into an important force for change. If the ideology, be it rational or magical, appeals to a wide enough segment of the population, it can create a broad enough power base to force government recognition.

Such an event has already occurred in New Guinea, where a "cargo cult" has provided the springboard for its leader to enter Parliament. To many people in the South Pacific, "cargo" is all those material items of Western origin whose manufacture they do not understand, and so have attributed to magical means. Cults have arisen which prophesy that members will receive cargo, and that they will gain control over national affairs. The emergence of cargo cults has been a direct response to the colonial situation, common to many islands in the South Pacific. Robert Trumbull wrote about the cults' political success in the New York *Times* on April 4, 1972:

YANGORU, Papua New Guinea—The leader of a "cargo cult" with headquarters in this remote jungle village has just been elected to the Papua New Guinea House of Assembly, or parliament, by an overwhelming vote.

As a member of the House, he may vote on such questions as when this vast Australian-administered territory of 2.5 million Melanesians, plus a few thousand whites and Chinese, will become self-governing and then independent.

The successful politician, Matthias Yaliwan, is said to have more than 60,000 followers who have paid to join the cult, which regards as sacred objects a used photographic flash cube and the gaudy cover of a paperback mystery by Agatha Christie.

Mr. Yaliwan gained widespread notoriety last year when he was reported to have proclaimed that human sacrifices would accompany the ceremonial uprooting of two cement survey markers placed on the summit of Mount Turu, near here, by a United States Air Force team in 1962.

The sacrifices were called off after Australian authorities exhibited interest, but thousands of credulous Melanesians followed Mr. Yaliwan to the 3,985-foot summit, considered a sacred place by animist villagers, in the belief that pulling up the markers would unlock a vast treasure deposited by ancestral spirits. The markers were pulled up, but the faithful believed that they had been tricked by the white man when no treasure was delivered.

VIEW THROUGH FLASH CUBE

Cargo cultists told a team of academic investigators from the University of Papua New Guinea that when they looked at the sacred mountain through the used flash cube, discarded by a newsman, they could "see the riches inside the mountain."

Veneration of the paperback cover of Miss Christie's

novel, "Evil Under the Sun," was thought by the university investigators to come from a confusion of the name Christie with Christ. Another theory cited in the academic study concerns the cover picture of a doll pierced with pins.

One of Mr. Yaliwan's lieutenants "believes that this persecuted lady is going to be the ruler of Papua New Guinea," the university report states.

But Mr. Yaliwan thinks that he himself is destined to be the leader of the country.

In an interview the 43-year-old former handyman declared in Pidgin, the English-based common language of the country, that his object in the House of Assembly would be to promote immediate independence and himself as "big fella leader o'long Papua New Guinea"—in other words, head of the Government.

Mr. Yaliwan's success in the election is seen as a measure of his cult's influence. A loser in the last election four years ago, he polled this time 7,200 votes to 435 for his nearest opponent in this jungle constituency.

The unprecedented success of this cargo cult transformed into a legislative force is based on the almost accidental discovery of the advantages of voluntary associations. Although drawn to the movement for the solutions it offers and the millennial prophecy, as Simpson describes, members soon discover that they must adhere to a formal organizational structure: maintaining an office, electing officials, and abiding by written rules and regulations. This gives them the opportunity to experiment politically and feel their own importance within a group, chances which would otherwise be denied them. So while members start by denying the relevance of established political structures, the nature of organizational life makes them a competing force within the political arena. At this point the crucial transformation takes place from a cult to an association that becomes attractive to larger numbers of people.

The lack of integration of many minority group members in the United States has given rise to groups which share some things with these movements. People are attracted to the Black Muslims and the Young Lords for their doctrines of radical and massive change and for the racial and ethnic iden-

tity it offers them. The movement then evolves a base of support within the community by developing task-oriented projects which meet the needs of the community. With this
broader base of community support, the movement then has
the choice of whether to act as an effective pressure group
within the larger political structure, or continue on a sepa-
ratist course.

---

9. THE RAS TAFARI MOVEMENT IN JAMAICA: A STUDY OF RACE AND CLASS CONFLICT

by George Eaton Simpson

The contra-acculturative aspects of Messianic cults and na-
tivistic movements have long been of interest to anthropologists and sociologists. Ras Tafari, a Jamaican cult which origi-
nated in 1930, is violently anti-white on the verbal level. Its
members regard Haile Selassie (Ras Tafari), Emperor of Abyssinia as the living God, see no hope for black men in the
British West Indies, and look forward to an early return to
Ethiopia.

The "Rasta" people consider Marcus Garvey, revered
founder of the Universal Negro Improvement Association, as
the forerunner of their movement. They claim that Garvey,
"the world's greatest statesman," was sent by Ras Tafari "to
cut and clear." Garvey advocated a mass migration to Africa,
and his slogans "Africa for the Africans—At Home and
Abroad" and "One God! One Aim! One Destiny!" are proclaimed at every Ras Tafari meeting.

In the early days of the movement, opposition came from
both the ordinary Jamaicans and the police. Lower class

Adapted from *Social Forces*, Volume 34, No. 2, December 1955,
pp. 167–70.

Jamaicans stoned speakers, slashed banners, and smashed lamps at street meetings. An active early leader of the cult was arrested, jailed, and tried seven times, but never convicted, on charges of disorderly conduct, ganja (marihuana) smoking, and lunacy. Open hostility to the movement has declined to some extent in recent years due, in part, to the well-disciplined control of members during meetings. Middle and upper class Jamaicans, as well as foreigners, still fear the Ras Tafarians, but available evidence does not support the widespread belief that they are bearded hoodlums.

Western Kingston and Eastern St. Andrew constitute the center of the Ras Tafari movement, but groups have been formed in other parts of the island. Participants are lower class Jamaicans, many of them unemployed or underemployed, who reside in crowded, blighted areas.

At present, twelve or fifteen Ras Tafari groups operate in Kingston and St. Andrew, with memberships ranging from twenty-five to one hundred and fifty or more. Groups form, split, and dissolve, and some individuals accept cult beliefs without attaching themselves to an organization. In contrast to a Revivalist group, which is dominated by a leader, a Ras Tafari band is extremely democratic. Everyone who wishes to speak must be heard, often at some length, and no action is taken without a vote of the membership, or, at the least, the executive committee. Names of these groups include: Ethiopian Coptic League, United Ethiopian Body, Ethiopian Youth Cosmic Fath, United Afro West Indian Federation, and African Cultural League.

BASIC DOCTRINES OF THE RAS TAFARI MOVEMENT

1. Ras Tafari (Haile Selassie) means "Lord Jehovah" or "Power of the Trinity." Haile Selassie is the only living King who is sitting on a throne, and he is on the throne of David. He is the King of Kings, the Lion of Judah, and the heads of other countries bow down before him. Proof of this assertion is found in such Biblical passages as Revelation 5:2,5— "And I saw a strong angel proclaiming with a loud voice, Who is worthy to open the book, and to loose the seals thereof? . . . And one of the elders saith unto me, Weep not; behold,

the Lion of Judah, the Root of David, hath prevailed to open the book, and to loose the seven spirits of God sent forth into all the earth."

2. Haile Selassie, with whom the Ras Tafarians have had no direct contact nor any correspondence, is believed to be invincible, even to the point of being the only one who can control the atomic bomb. The proof offered for this claim is a picture of the Emperor of Abyssinia standing with one foot on a large unexploded bomb at the time his country was invaded by Italian forces.

3. Black men are Ethiopians. They are the true Israelites, once the greatest people in the world. God is black, Christ was black, Solomon was black, and black Jamaicans are reincarnations of the ancient Hebrews. Residence in the West Indies is punishment for past stubbornness and transgression. However, black men have now suffered enough and it is time for them to go home.

4. The Romans made idols of wood and stone, stood them up and worshipped them. The English thought that was too simple, so they invented the idea that God is a spirit in Heaven that men cannot see. Since white men have given no proof to support this belief, it can only be regarded as a racket. Ras Tafari is the living God.

5. Heaven is an invention of the white man which is used to deceive black men by promising them everything after death. Since dead men tell no tales, there is no proof of the existence of the Englishman's Heaven. Ethiopia is the only real heaven.

RAS TAFARI MEETINGS

Most Ras Tafari bands hold one meeting at their headquarters and two street meetings weekly. A typical Sunday night meeting in the leader's yard consists mainly of speeches expounding the doctrines of the movement interspersed with the singing of original songs and modified Sankey and Methodist hymns. Examples of the latter include "Let the Song Go Round the Earth," "Beulah Land," and "From Greenland's Icy Mountains." The words of one of the favorite original compositions are:

Here We Are in this Land

Here we are in this land.
No one think how we stand
The hands that are on us all day.
So we cry and we sigh
For we know not our God.
So we always be crying in vain.

Our forefathers cried;
Feel the pangs of the chain
See the blood running out of his vein.
And our slave masters did pierce
Our forefathers' hearts
So they die like a brute in the chain.

These meetings end with the singing of the Ethiopian national anthem and the recitation of the Ethiopian prayer, both composed in Western Kingston. The prayer ends with the words: "Deliver us from the hands of our enemies that we might prove fruitful for the last days. When our enemies are passed and decayed in the depths of the sea, in the depths of the earth, or in the belly of a beast, Oh give us all a place in Thy Kingdom for ever and ever. Selah."

Special meetings are occasionally held, especially in November on the anniversary of Haile Selassie's coronation. On such occasions, the special decorations, music, and refreshments, and the dedication of babies to Ras Tafari, attract a large assembly.

SIX RAS TAFARI THEMES

In private conversations, small group discussions, regular meetings and street meetings, six constantly recurring themes appear, namely: The Wickedness of the White Man; The Superiority of the Black Man; Jamaica's False Prophets; The Hopelessness of the Jamaican Situation for Black Men; Revenge; and Africa, the Homeland, Is Heaven and the Only Hope for the Black Man.

The Wickedness of the White Man. According to this theme, white slave masters were murderers and criminals. A favorite saying is that during slavery, the white man killed the baby of a black woman and said: "Mary Jane, go back to work." Today the white man accuses the black man of being a thief, but the white man has stolen continents and men. White men of today are hypocrites, murderers, and criminal thieves, and they cannot escape responsibility for what happened in the past because the tree bears fruit and the seeds of the fruit become trees (the doctrine of reincarnation).

The Superiority of the Black Man. Black men were civilized when the white man was living in the caves of northern Europe. The throne of Ethiopia is older than the throne of St. George. The white man says that black men are no good, but David, Solomon, and the Queen of Sheba were black. The knowledge black men have cannot be obtained in college. They are born with the knowledge they possess because they have been with God from the beginning of Creation, and they have been with God everywhere. They have been through these things before. The white man cannot beat them on history. The white man lies, but black men can contradict everything he says. The white man tells black men they are inferior, but they are not inferior. They are superior and the white man is inferior.

Jamaica's False Prophets. The two wickedest kinds of men are the preachers and the police. The fraud of religion and politics have kept black men in ignorance and have kept them back. The church robs men, not of their pockets, but of their mentality. Because of the church, the black man in Jamaica is concerned more with death than with life. School teachers never teach black men anything but foolishness, and black men want no more of the white man's indoctrination. Everything about the white man is false.

The Hopelessness of the Jamaican Situation for Black Men. The Jamaican Government, the worst government in the world, is corrupt and nothing can be expected from it. The politicians are out only for themselves; they want your vote and nothing else. Bustamante and Manley (leaders of the two principal political parties in Jamaica) are as bad as the other (English) politicians. Black men are slaves today, and their slavery is worse than that during the days of slavery because they are mentally enslaved. The white man keeps black men in poverty. "It is like being in prison, and there will be no freedom until we go back home."

Revenge. "We understand what the white man has done to us and we are going to do unto them as they have done unto us. In Ethiopia, the white man will have to serve us." Isaiah 14 says: ". . . and the house of Israel shall possess them [the strangers] in the land of the Lord for servants and handmaids; and they shall take them captives, whose captives they were; and they shall rule over their oppressors." Mau Mau is a war between black men and white men, and the Mau Mau are angels of deliverance sent by Haile Selassie to drive white men out of Africa. Ras Tafari says: "Death to the white man and to the black traitors." Today it is nation against nation, and the time is short. The King of Israel shall rule over all, and anyone who stands in the way, including the big, fat Negroes (middle class Jamaicans), will be removed; there will be a remission of blood.

Africa, the Homeland, Is Heaven and the Only Hope for the Black Man. The Chinese have a native land—China, and the Indian has his native land—India. The black man has his native land too—Ethiopia. "The white man tells us to wait until Jesus comes, but we're not going to wait. In the near future, we are going back to our Homeland. The only future for the black man is with Ras Tafari. Our God and Our King is here to deliver us, and when we go back to that land no one will ever get us again." . . .

FUNCTIONS AND DYSFUNCTIONS OF THE RAS TAFARI MOVEMENT

The social psychological functions of the Ras Tafari movement, like those of esoteric cults in general, include: compensation for the humiliations and deprivations of a lowly social station; emotional warmth and friendship of the leader and like-minded believers; hope for a better life in the otherworld; recreation; opportunities for self-expression through singing, speech-making, procession-leading, and costume-wearing; recognition through office-holding or as a speaker, musician, organizer or fund-raiser; and economic assistance at

PART III

PROBLEMS IN MENTAL HEALTH

The selections in Part III illustrate the application anthropological studies can have in rethinking one kind of bureaucracy—that of mental health. The kinds of societies anthropologists usually study lack the high degree of specialization which, in urban settings, leads to discrepancies between the goals of agencies and the goals of the people they serve.

One of the ways in which bureaucracies become unresponsive is by losing touch with the priorities of the people. The community mental health movement arose because of bureaucratic failure to reach and treat people without disturbing their social networks drastically. For example, receiving mental hospitals send patients hundreds of miles from their homes for long term care, making it impossible to maintain family relationships. Although aftercare may be available close to the patient's home, he is often sent to the other end of the city for bureaucratic convenience.

The community mental health movement also set out to do preventive work—helping people deal with problems such as suicidal feelings and marital conflict before people have to be hospitalized. An attempt was made to be the place close by where people could go to talk about things that were bothering them, in a center that belonged to them. Unfortunately, community mental health centers have too often developed along the same lines as hospitals, offering the same kinds of impersonal and cursory care.

The problem of defining community proved to be a big stumbling block: each center was arbitrarily assigned a geographical area, and people in the "catchment area" had to be told that it existed and taught how to use it. Perhaps the biggest problem with this concept of community is that the centers did not grow out of initiative on the part of the people they were to serve. In a city, the only workable definition of community may be the reaching out of people together, and not an arbitrary geographical area. Anthropologists study community as a central principle in how people live; this makes their work especially useful to those who look to community as a way of reorganizing institutions such as departments of social services, boards of education, and housing authorities.

The involvement and participation of people in their own treatment in Yoruba and Ojibwa cultures illustrates a close cooperation among patient, family, and healer which would be of great use in counteracting urban alienation. But stresses caused by the failure of schools, families, and jobs to meet people's needs cannot be remedied singlehandedly by such agencies as community mental health centers, no matter how responsive and enlightened they may become. People can and do take the initiative in forming groups to fill "service gaps." New structures must be incorporated into city life to facilitate the seizing of initiative and participation in the decisions that affect people's lives.

Mental health workers deal in categories. The anthropological perspective suggests that they rethink these categories in the light of cultural and subcultural influences on mental illness. The black person who complains that he is a victim of covert discrimination may now be referred to the Human Rights Commission, while twenty years ago he would have more likely been diagnosed as having possible paranoid tendencies. This example shows how changes in the values of our own culture make us look at subcultures differently.

Introduction to
Anthropology and the Abnormal

Cultural relativism challenges the standard medical model of what is normal and what is abnormal. This approach has important implications for both research and treatment. If the assumption is that abnormal behavior is that which is not supported by the values of a culture, abnormality can only be defined within a culture—this makes it very hard to compare or evaluate mental illness from one culture to another.

The position that abnormal behavior is due to cultural stress, rather than individual weakness of character or constitution, suggests a dual approach to treatment. Changing the society which causes undue stress is as important as fortifying the patient against those stresses in his life. Most professional training concentrates on the latter, but current challenges to the mental health field are bringing the need to work for social change into greater prominence.

Benedict proposes the ideal that people interested in cultural differences suspend their own values and judgments in order to understand others completely on their own terms. This is never completely possible, since we are all socialized to some set of values, and are bound to have emotional reactions to behavior which goes against them.

Value judgments can interfere with a full understanding of another culture, but so can focusing on one aspect of a culture to the exclusion of others. Benedict interprets the potlatch custom primarily in psychological terms, but recent studies have shown that it has the important economic function of redistributing food from areas which have more to those which have less. Far from undermining the psychological insights Benedict offers, these findings suggest other uses the potlatch has for Northwest Coast American Indians, thus rounding out the multiple meanings this institution has.

10. ANTHROPOLOGY AND THE ABNORMAL

by Ruth Benedict

. . . one of the most striking facts that emerge from a study
of widely varying cultures is the ease with which our abnormals function in other cultures. It does not matter what kind
of "abnormality" we choose for illustration, those which indicate extreme instability, or those which are more in the nature
of character traits like sadism or delusions of grandeur or of
persecution, there are well-described cultures in which these
abnormals function at ease and with honor, and apparently
without danger or difficulty to the society.

The most notorious of these is trance and catalepsy. Even
a very mild mystic is aberrant in our culture. But most peoples
have regarded even extreme psychic manifestations not only
as normal and desirable, but even as characteristic of highly
valued and gifted individuals. This was true even in our own
cultural background in that period when Catholicism made
the ecstatic experience the mark of sainthood. It is hard for
us, born and brought up in a culture that makes no use of
the experience, to realize how important a rôle it may play
and how many individuals are capable of it, once it has been
given an honorable place in any society.

Some of the Indian tribes of California accorded prestige
principally to those who passed through certain trance experiences. Not all of these tribes believed that it was exclusively
women who were so blessed, but among the Shasta this was
the convention. Their shamans were women, and they were
accorded the greatest prestige in the community. They were
chosen because of their constitutional liability to trance and
allied manifestations. One day the woman who was so des-

Adapted from *Journal of General Psychology*, Volume 10, 1934, pp.
59–79.

tined, while she was about her usual work, would fall suddenly to the ground. She had heard a voice speaking to her in tones of the greatest intensity. Turning, she had seen a man with drawn bow and arrow. He commanded her to sing on pain of being shot through the heart by his arrow, but under the stress of the experience she fell senseless. Her family gathered. She was lying rigid, hardly breathing. They knew that for some time she had had dreams of a special character which indicated a shamanistic calling, dreams of escaping grizzly bears, falling off cliffs or trees, or of being surrounded by swarms of yellow jackets. The community knew therefore what to expect. After a few hours the woman began to moan gently and to roll about upon the ground, trembling violently. She was supposed to be repeating the song which she had been told to sing and which during the trance had been taught her by the spirit. As she revived her moaning became more and more clearly the spirit's song until at last she called out the name of the spirit itself, and immediately blood oozed from her mouth.

When the woman had come to herself after the first encounter with her spirit she danced that night her first initiatory shamanistic dance, holding herself by a rope that was swung from the ceiling. For three nights she danced, and on the third night she had to receive in her body her power from her spirit. She was dancing, and as she felt the approach of the moment she called out, "He will shoot me, he will shoot me." Her friends stood close, for when she reeled in a kind of cataleptic seizure, they had to seize her before she fell or she would die. From this time on she had in her body a visible materialization of her spirit's power, an icicle-like object which in her dances thereafter she would exhibit, producing it from one part of her body and returning it to another part. From this time on she continued to validate her supernatural power by further cataleptic demonstrations, and she was called upon in great emergencies of life and death, for curing and for divination and for counsel. She became in other words by this procedure a woman of great power and importance.

It is clear that, so far from regarding cataleptic seizures as blots upon the family escutcheon and as evidences of dreaded disease, cultural approval had seized upon them and made of them the pathway to authority over one's fellows. They were the outstanding characteristic of the most respected social type, the type which functioned with most honor and reward in the community. It was precisely the cataleptic individuals who in this culture were singled out for authority and leadership.

The availability of "abnormal" types in the social structure, provided they are types that are culturally selected by that group, is illustrated from every part of the world. The shamans of Siberia dominate their communities. According to the ideas of these peoples, they are individuals who by submission to the will of the spirits have been cured of a grievous illness—the onset of the seizures—and have acquired by this means great supernatural power and incomparable vigor and health. Some, during the period of the call, are violently insane for several years, others irresponsible to the point where they have to be watched constantly lest they wander off in the snow and freeze to death, others ill and emaciated to the point of death, sometimes with bloody sweat. It is the shamanistic practice which constitutes their cure, and the extreme physical exertion of a Siberian seance leaves them, they claim, rested and able to enter immediately upon a similar performance. Cataleptic seizures are regarded as an essential part of any shamanistic performance.

A good description of the neurotic condition of the shaman and the attention given him by his society is an old one by Canon Callaway recorded in the words of an old Zulu of South Africa:

The condition of a man who is about to become a diviner is this; at first he is apparently robust, but in the process of time he begins to be delicate, not having any real disease, but being delicate. He habitually avoids certain kinds of food, choosing what he likes, and he does not eat much of that; he is continually complaining of pains in different parts of his body. And he tells them that he has dreamt that he was carried away by a river. He dreams of many things, and his body is muddied (as a river) and he becomes a house of dreams. He dreams constantly of many things, and on awaking tells his friends, "My body is muddied today; I dreamt many men were killing me, and I escaped I know not how. On waking one part of my body felt different from other parts; it was no longer alike all over." At last that man is very ill, and they go to the diviners to enquire.

The diviners do not at once see that he is about to have a soft head (that is, the sensitivity associated with shamanism). It is difficult for them to see the truth; they continually talk nonsense and make false statements, until all the man's cattle are devoured at their command, they saying that the spirit of his people demands cattle, that it may eat food. At length all the man's property is expended, he still being ill; and they no longer know what to do, for he has no more cattle, and his friends help him in such things as he needs.

At length a diviner comes and says that all the others are wrong. He says, "He is possessed by the spirits. There is nothing else. They move in him, being divided into two parties; some say, 'No, we do not wish our child injured. We do not wish it.' It is for that reason he does not get well. If you bar the way against the spirits, you will be killing him. For he will not be a diviner; neither will he ever be a man again."

So the man may be ill two years without getting better; perhaps even longer than that. He is confined to his house. This continues till his hair falls off. And his body is dry and scurfy; he does not like to anoint himself. He shows that he is about to be a diviner by yawning again and again, and by sneezing continually. It is apparent also from his being very fond of snuff; not allowing any long time to pass without taking some. And people begin to see that he has had what is good given to him.

After that he is ill; he has convulsions, and when water has been poured on him they then cease for a time. He habitually sheds tears, at first slight, then at last he weeps aloud and when the people are asleep he is heard making a noise and wakes the people by his singing; he has composed a song, and the men and women awake and go to sing in concert with him. All the people of the village are troubled by want of sleep; for a man who is becoming a diviner causes great trouble, for he does not sleep, but works constantly with his brain; his sleep is merely by snatches, and he wakes up singing many songs; and people who are near quit their villages by night when they hear him singing aloud and go to sing in concert. Perhaps he sings till morning, no one having slept. And then he leaps about the house like a frog; and the house becomes too small for him, and he goes out leaping and singing, and shaking like a reed in the water, and dripping with perspiration.

In this state of things they daily expect his death; he is now but skin and bones, and they think that tomorrow's sun will not leave him alive. At this time many cattle are eaten, for the people encourage his becoming a diviner. At length (in a dream) an ancient ancestral spirit is pointed out to him. This spirit says to him, "Go to So-and-so and he will churn for you an emetic (the medicine the drinking of which is a part of shamanistic initiation) that you may be a diviner altogether." Then he is quiet a few days, having gone to the diviner to have the medicine churned for him; and he comes back quite another man, being now cleansed and a diviner indeed.

Thereafter for life when he achieves possession, he foretells events, and finds lost articles.

It is clear that culture may value and make socially available even highly unstable human types. If it chooses to treat their peculiarities as the most valued variants of human behavior, the individuals in question will rise to the occasion and perform their social rôles without reference to our usual ideas of the types who can make social adjustments and those who cannot.

Cataleptic and trance phenomena are, of course, only one illustration of the fact that those whom we regard as abnormals may function adequately in other cultures. Many of our culturally discarded traits are selected for elaboration in different societies. Homosexuality is an excellent example, for in this case our attention is not constantly diverted, as in the consideration of trance, to the interruption of routine activity which it implies. Homosexuality poses the problem very simply. A tendency toward this trait in our culture exposes an individual to all the conflicts to which all aberrants are always exposed, and we tend to identify the consequences of this conflict with homosexuality. But these consequences are obviously local and cultural. Homosexuals in many societies are not incompetent, but they may be such if the culture asks adjustments of them that would strain any man's vitality.

Wherever homosexuality has been given an honorable place in any society, those to whom it is congenial have filled adequately the honorable rôles society assigns to them. Plato's *Republic* is, of course, the most convincing statement of such a reading of homosexuality. It is presented as one of the major means to the good life, and it was generally so regarded in Greece at that time.

The cultural attitude toward homosexuals has not always been on such a high ethical plane, but it has been very varied. Among many American Indian tribes there exists the institution of the berdache, as the French called them. These men-women were men who at puberty or thereafter took the dress and the occupations of women. Sometimes they married other men and lived with them. Sometimes they were men with no inversion, persons of weak sexual endowment who chose this rôle to avoid the jeers of the women. The berdaches were never regarded as of first-rate supernatural power, as similar men-women were in Siberia, but rather as leaders in women's occupations, good healers in certain diseases, or, among certain tribes, as the genial organizers of social affairs. In any case, they were socially placed. They were not left exposed to the conflicts that visit the deviant who is excluded from participation in the recognized patterns of his society.

The most spectacular illustrations of the extent to which normality may be culturally defined are those cultures where an abnormality of our culture is the cornerstone of their social structure. It is not possible to do justice to these possibilities in a short discussion. A recent study of an island of northwest Melanesia by Fortune describes a society built upon traits which we regard as beyond the border of paranoia. In this tribe the exogamic groups look upon each other as prime manipulators of black magic, so that one marries always into an enemy group which remains for life one's deadly and unappeasable foes. They look upon a good garden crop as a confession of theft, for everyone is engaged in making magic to induce into his garden the productiveness of his neighbors'; therefore no secrecy in the island is so rigidly insisted upon as the secrecy of a man's harvesting of his yams. Their polite phrase at the acceptance of a gift is, "And if you now poison me, how shall I repay you this present?" Their preoccupation with poisoning is constant; no woman ever leaves her cooking pot for a moment untended. Even the great affinal economic exchanges that are characteristic of this Melanesian culture area are quite altered in Dobu since they are incompatible with this fear and distrust that pervades the culture. They go farther and people the whole world outside their own quarters with such malignant spirits that all-night feasts and ceremonials simply do not occur here. They have even rigorous religiously enforced customs that forbid the sharing of seed even in one family group. Anyone else's food is deadly poison to you, so that communality of stores is out of the question. For some months before harvest the whole society is on the verge of starvation, but if one falls to the temptation and eats up one's seed yams, one is an outcast and a beachcomber for life. There is no coming back. It involves, as a matter of course, divorce and the breaking of all social ties.

Now in this society where no one may work with another and no one may share with another, Fortune describes the individual who was regarded by all his fellows as crazy. He was not one of those who periodically ran amok and, beside himself and frothing at the mouth, fell with a knife upon anyone he could reach. Such behavior they did not regard as putting anyone outside the pale. They did not even put the individuals who were known to be liable to these attacks under any kind of control. They merely fled when they saw the attack coming on and kept out of the way. "He would be all right tomorrow." But there was one man of sunny, kindly disposition who liked work and liked to be helpful. The compulsion was too strong for him to repress it in favor of the opposite tendencies of his culture. Men and women never spoke of him without laughing; he was silly and simple and definitely crazy. Nevertheless, to the ethnologist used to a culture that has, in Christianity, made his type the model of all virtue, he seemed a pleasant fellow.

An even more extreme example, because it is of a culture that has built itself upon a more complex abnormality, is that of the North Pacific Coast of North America. The civilization of the Kwakiutl, at the time when it was first recorded in the last decades of the nineteenth century, was one of the most vigorous in North America. It was built up on an ample economic supply of goods, the fish which furnished their food staple being practically inexhaustible and obtainable with comparatively small labor, and the wood which furnished the material for their houses, their furnishings, and their arts being, with however much labor, always procurable. They lived in coastal villages that compared favorably in size with those of any other American Indians and they kept up constant communication by means of seagoing dug-out canoes.

It was one of the most vigorous and zestful of the aboriginal cultures of North America, with complex crafts and ceremonials, and elaborate and striking arts. It certainly had none of the earmarks of a sick civilization. The tribes of the Northwest Coast had wealth, and exactly in our terms. That is, they had not only a surplus of economic goods, but they made a game of the manipulation of wealth. It was by no means a mere direct transcription of economic needs and the filling of those needs. It involved the idea of capital, of interest, and of conspicuous waste. It was a game with all the binding rules of a game, and a person entered it as a child. His father distributed wealth for him, according to his ability, at a small feast or potlatch, and each gift the receiver was obliged to accept and to return after a short interval with interest that ran to about 100 per cent a year. By the time the child was grown, therefore, he was well launched, a larger potlatch had been given for him on various occasions of exploit or initiation, and he had wealth either out at usury or in his own possession. Nothing in the civilization could be enjoyed without validating it by the distribution of this wealth. Everything that was valued, names and songs as well as material objects, were passed down in family lines, but they were always publicly assumed with accompanying sufficient distributions of property. It was the game of validating and exercising all the privileges one could accumulate from one's various forbears, or by gift, or by marriage, that made the chief interest of the culture. Everyone in his degree took part in it, but many, of course, mainly as spectators. In its highest form it was played out between rival chiefs representing not only themselves and their family lines but their communities, and the object of the contest was to glorify oneself and to humiliate one's opponent. On this level of greatness the property involved was no longer represented by blankets, so many thousand of them to a potlatch, but by higher units of value. These higher units were like our bank notes. They were incised copper tablets, each of them named, and having a value that depended upon their illustrious history. This was as high as ten thousand blankets, and to possess one of them, still more to enhance its value at a great potlatch, was one of the greatest glories within the compass of the chiefs of the Northwest Coast.

The details of this manipulation of wealth are in many ways a parody on our own economic arrangements, but it is with the motivations that were recognized in this contest that we are concerned in this discussion. The drives were those which in our own culture we should call megalomaniac. There was an uncensored self-glorification and ridicule of the opponent that it is hard to equal in other cultures outside of the monologues of the abnormal. Any of the songs and speeches of their chiefs at a potlatch illustrate the usual tenor:

I am the only great tree, I the chief.
I am the only great tree, I the chief.
You are my subordinates, tribes.
You sit in the middle of the rear of the house, tribes.
Bring me your counter of property, tribes, that he may in vain try to count what is going to be given away by the great copper-maker, the chief.
Oh, I laugh at them, I sneer at them who empty boxes in their houses, their potlatch houses, their inviting houses that are full only of hunger. They follow along after me like young sawbill ducks. I am the only great tree, I the chief.

I have quoted . . . these hymns of self-glorification because by an association which psychiatrists will recognize as fundamental these delusions of grandeur were essential in the paranoid view of life which was so strikingly developed in this culture. All of existence was seen in terms of insult. Not only derogatory acts performed by a neighbor or an enemy, but all untoward events, like a cut when one's axe slipped, or a ducking when one's canoe overturned, were insults. All alike threatened first and foremost one's ego security, and the first thought one was allowed was how to get even, how to wipe out the insult. Grief was little institutionalized, but sulking took its place. Until he had resolved upon a course of action by which to save his face after any misfortune, whether it was the slipping of a wedge in felling a tree, or the death of a favorite child, an Indian of the Northwest Coast retired to his pallet with his face to the wall and neither ate nor spoke. He rose from it to follow out some course which according to the traditional rules should reinstate him in his own eyes and those of the community: to distribute property enough to wipe out the stain, or to go headhunting in order that somebody else should be made to mourn. His activities in neither case were specific responses to the bereavement he had just passed through, but were elaborately directed toward getting even. If he had not the money to distribute and did not succeed in killing someone to humiliate another, he might take his own life. He had staked everything, in his view of life, upon a certain picture of the self, and, when the bubble of his self-esteem was pricked, he had no interest, no occupation to fall back on, and the collapse of his inflated ego left him prostrate.

Every contingency of life was dealt with in these two traditional ways. To them the two were equivalent. Whether one fought with weapons or "fought with property," as they say, the same idea was at the bottom of both. In the olden times, they say, they fought with spears, but now they fight with property. One overcomes one's opponents in equivalent fashion in both, matching forces and seeing that one comes out ahead, and one can thumb one's nose at the vanquished rather more satisfactorily at a potlatch than on a battle field. Every occasion in life was noticed, not in its own terms, as a stage in the sex life of the individual or as a climax of joy or of grief, but as furthering this drama of consolidating one's own prestige and bringing shame to one's guests. Whether it was the occasion of the birth of a child, or a daughter's adolescence, or of the marriage of one's son, they were all equivalent raw material for the culture to use for this one traditionally selected end. They were all to raise one's own personal status and to entrench oneself by the humiliation of one's fellows. A girl's adolescence among the Nootka was an event for which her father gathered property from the time she was first able to run about. When she was adolescent he would demonstrate his greatness by an unheard of distribution of these goods, and put down all his rivals. It was not as a fact of the girl's sex life that it figured in their culture, but as the occasion for a major move in the great game of vindicating one's own greatness and humiliating one's associates.

In their behavior at great bereavements this set of the culture comes out most strongly. Among the Kwakiutl it did not matter whether a relative had died in bed of disease, or by the hand of an enemy, in either case death was an affront to be wiped out by the death of another person. The fact that one had been caused to mourn was proof that one had been put upon. A chief's sister and her daughter had gone up to Victoria, and either because they drank bad whiskey or because their boat capsized they never came back. The chief called together his warriors. "Now I ask you, tribes, who shall wail? Shall I do it or shall another?" The spokesman answered, of course, "Not you, Chief. Let some other of the tribes." Immediately they set up the war pole to announce their intention of wiping out the injury, and gathered a war party. They set out, and found seven men and two children asleep and killed them. "Then they felt good when they arrived at Sebaa in the evening."

The point which is of interest to us is that in our society those who on that occasion would feel good when they arrived at Sebaa that evening would be the definitely abnormal. There would be some, even in our society, but it is not a recognized and approved mood under the circumstances. On the Northwest Coast those are favored and fortunate to whom that mood under those circumstances is congenial, and those to whom it is repugnant are unlucky. This latter minority can register in their own culture only by doing violence to their congenial responses and acquiring others that are difficult for them. The person, for instance, who, like a Plains Indian whose wife has been taken from him, is too proud to fight, can deal with the Northwest Coast civilization only by ignoring its strongest bents. If he cannot achieve it, he is the deviant in that culture, their instance of abnormality.

This head-hunting that takes place on the Northwest Coast after a death is no matter of blood revenge or of organized vengeance. There is no effort to tie up the subsequent killing with any responsibility on the part of the victim for the death of the person who is being mourned. A chief whose son has died goes visiting wherever his fancy dictates, and he says to his host, "My prince has died today, and you go with him." Then he kills him. In this, according to their interpretation, he acts nobly because he has not been downed. He has thrust back in return. The whole procedure is meaningless without the fundamental paranoid reading of bereavement. Death, like all the other untoward accidents of existence, confounds man's pride and can only be handled in the category of insults.

Behavior honored upon the Northwest Coast is one which is recognized as abnormal in our civilization, and yet it is sufficiently close to the attitudes of our own culture to be intelligible to us and to have a definite vocabulary with which we may discuss it. The megalomaniac paranoid trend is a definite danger in our society. It is encouraged by some of our major preoccupations, and it confronts us with a choice of two possible attitudes. One is to brand it as abnormal and reprehensible, and is the attitude we have chosen in our civilization. The other is to make it an essential attribute of ideal man, and this is the solution in the culture of the Northwest Coast. . . .

Introduction to
Ojibwa World View and Disease

The Ojibwa Indians of North America believe that illness is the punishment for wrongdoing, which makes disease function as a form of social control in a society where there is no police force or army. Community norms are enforced by fear of disease. While most Western cultures do not consciously believe that illness is a punishment for sin, some of their institutions seem to reflect that belief in their use of isolation and punitive methods of treatment. In fact, social control is a main function of those mental hospitals in our society which offer little but custodial care. Mental institutions enforce a certain range of acceptable behavior by applying sanctions: they keep disturbing people off the streets and serve as alternatives to jail.

The Ojibwa believe that a person who does wrong causes illness to others within the family. The treatment procedure restores equilibrium to the family unity—the family must call in the healer, attend the confession, and pay the fee. This teaches norms to children and discourages deviation.

While Hallowell uses the term "confession," the public Ojibwa ceremony is very different from the private penance and restoration of grace in Christianity. There is a parallel here to family therapy in that one family member's problems may precipitate therapy, but the whole family is seen as involved. Treating the whole family is a beginning in recognizing the role of social and cultural interactions in the cause and cure of mental illness.

11. OJIBWA WORLD VIEW AND DISEASE
by A. Irving Hallowell

. . . Within Ojibwa society, macroscopic—social or public procedures—for punishment are absent. No institutionalized means exist for the public adjudication of disputes or conflict of any kind. There is no council of elders or any forum in which judgment can be passed upon the conduct of individuals. There is no way in which publicly sanctioned punishment can be initiated in cases of incest, murder, or any other offense. Children, it is true, are disciplined by their parents but corporal punishment is rare. But in the social world of adults there are no superordinate modes of social control, no institutionalized means of punishment. . . .

In the absence, then, of public procedures with sanctioning functions, or a belief in the punishing roles of other-than-human persons, it is apparent that if social sanctions are to operate at all, they must be intimately linked with motivations that are connected with a sense of moral responsibility for conduct mediated through ego and superego functions. In order to understand how a disease sanction effectively reinforces the basic values of Ojibwa culture, there are several factors that must be taken into account, besides the affective states provoked by the illness.

Every individual is not only assumed to be morally responsible for his conduct: in disease situations that arouse anxiety he is also forced to become the judge of his own past conduct. Feelings of guilt become particularly acute when it is understood that infants, too young to be penalized for their own

Adapted from "Ojibwa World View and Disease" by A. Irving Hallowell, Man's Image in Medicine and Anthropology, Monograph IV, edited by Iago Galdston, M.D., International University Press Inc., New York, 1963, pp. 258–315.

ad conduct, may be suffering because of the past misconduct of their parents. Thus, whether I become ill or my children do, the question arises: What have *I* done that was wrong? With the help of a doctor, I have to answer this question concretely. I have to reflect on my past behavior. I have to think about my relations with other persons, both human and other-than-human. It is necessary that I identify the bad conduct that has followed me, even if I have to go back to my childhood. I have to pass judgment on my own conduct.

It is useless to withhold anything, because the doctor, with the aid of his other-than-human helpers, will probably find out what kind of bad conduct has followed me. Consequently, the discovery and articulation of it become equivalent to a *confession* of wrongdoing. This is an essential step, necessary to promote recovery. Medicine can then do its work. Thus, confession adds considerable psychological force to the disease sanction. In order to get well, the individual has to suffer not only guilt, but the shame of exposure involved in confession—although this may relieve some of his anxiety.

Confession is also the means by which knowledge of concrete cases of bad conduct is put into social circulation. For, among the Ojibwa, there is no isolation of a patient; on the contrary, the wigwam is always full of people. Any statement on the part of the patient, although it may be made to the doctor, is actually *public* knowledge, and may very quickly become a matter of common gossip. Under these conditions, to confess a transgression is to publicly reveal what may be a secret "sin." To the Ojibwa, however, this public exposure is important. The very secrecy of misconduct is bad in itself, as, for examples, covert aggression through witchcraft, or sexual transgressions. Once misconduct has been publicized, it is washed away, or, as the Ojibwa phrase it, "bad conduct will not follow you any more." When one participant in sexual misconduct confesses, the other person will not subsequently become ill or have to confess.

Confession, by making secret misconduct public, places the sick person on the road to recovery. This is its ostensible purpose, as viewed by the Ojibwa themselves. But confession also has a wider, *social* function: children growing up in Ojibwa society come to *sense*, even if they do not fully understand, the general typology of disapproved conduct. At the same time, since patients who confess often recover, the publicity given to such cases supports both the Ojibwa explanation of serious illness and the efficacy of confession itself. So, while most individuals are motivated to avoid the risk of illness, there is, perhaps, consolation in the fact that even if bad conduct does follow you, there still is an available means of regaining health. . . .

Interpersonal relations between human beings and other-than-human persons. I have pointed out that persons of the other-than-human class are expected to share their knowledge and power with human beings, so that their "social" role in the Ojibwa universe is defined as essentially rewarding, rather than punitive. It is particularly important that men obtain "blessings" from the persons of this class; that is the purpose of the aboriginal puberty fast, in which boys come "face to face" with other-than-human persons in dreams or visions. The blessings gained range from invulnerability to bullets to the acquisition of specialized curing powers. What kind of bad conduct, then, can become the source of illness, and what kinds of values are reinforced by the application of a disease sanction to the relationship between human and other-than-human persons? . . .

The commands of the [other-than-human persons] are absolute, though the obligations they impose may take various forms. There may be a food tabu in cases where the "masters" of particular species of game animals share their power; e.g., one man was forbidden to kill or eat porcupine by the "master" of the porcupines. . . .

In another case, a man was commanded to wear the kind of headgear attributed to a certain mythical character, so it was inferred that this "person" was one of his "guardian spirits." Another man was forbidden to speak to or have sexual intercourse with his wife for a defined period after marriage.

Such obligations are never talked about because there is a general tabu on any references to the relations of a man and his "dream visitors," except under unusual circumstances. So, the observances of the imposed commands often require the firmest self-discipline, for behavior that is not always intelligible to others, and cannot be explained to them, is involved.

The man who was not permitted to sleep with his wife or even talk to her did not succeed in fulfilling his obligation. His wife did not understand his conduct, and left him after one winter of married life. He married again and this time broke the tabu. One of his children became sick and died; later his wife died. He married a third time and the same thing happened. It was useless for him to expect [harmony]; he had received a "blessing," but had not been able to exercise sufficient self-control to benefit by it.

Food tabus are interpreted so rigidly that inadvertent, or unconscious violations do not modify the penalty for their infraction. In these cases, as in others, I not only lose my "blessing," but endanger my health and that of my family. Furthermore, the wrongdoing that follows me when I have violated an obligation to other-than-human persons eventuates in illness that cannot be cured. The linguistic term applied to such infractions means: "failure to observe an obligation earnestly entered into."

Penalization of failure to meet such obligations not only emphasizes the moral relations between human and other-than-human persons; I think we can infer that it also underlines the generic importance of the moral responsibility which the Ojibwa individual is expected to assume for his conduct in *all* interpersonal relations. In the case of men, it also epitomizes the relation between the vital need that is felt for the help of other-than-human persons in the Ojibwa world, and the need for the self-discipline that is required to achieve [harmony], not only for one's self but for one's family.

There is a connection between the psychological reinforcement of self-discipline, moral responsibility, and the stark realities that inhere in a hunting and fishing economy. Self-discipline underlies the self-reliance that is required of the hunter. An illness which is thought to eventuate from the violation of moral obligations to "our grandfathers" cannot be interpreted as stemming from their anger. *They* have done what they could for me; they have fulfilled their role. On my side, I must be able to accept obligations and fulfill them if I wish to reap the benefit of the help I have been offered by them. Among other things, self-discipline is necessary. The severity of the disease sanction in such cases is psychologically sound, if it is interpreted as a means of reinforcing motivations connected with self-discipline, for the Ojibwa are a people for whom life is fraught with objective hazards, which are inescapable. At the same time the sanction lends support, in principle, to moral responsibility for conduct in *all* interpersonal relations. Interdependence and cooperation is vital for survival. Human beings *can* obtain vital help in meeting the hazards of life from other-than-human persons so long as they fulfill the obligation imposed by "our grandfathers." Knowing this, a sense of security is fostered.

What are the limits to the knowledge and power an individual may acquire from other-than-human persons? A case I was told about indicates that there are certain traditional limits recognized. Greediness for power, to the extent that it might enable an individual to far outclass his fellow men, is negatively sanctioned. The case in point involved the puberty fast of a boy who was not satisfied with his initial "blessings." He wanted to dream of all the leaves of all the trees in the world so that absolutely nothing would be hidden from him. While the "dream visitor" granted his desire, the boy did not live to benefit by it. He was told that "as soon as the leaves start to fall you'll get sick, and when all the leaves drop to the ground, that is the end of your life."

"Over-dreaming," or "over-fasting," as it has been called, is evaluated as particularly selfish. Trying to obtain more power than is actually necessary for living is the moral equivalent of hoarding material things, like food. It violates the principle that no one should have too much of anything. All that one really needs is what can be put to use in the foreseeable future. On the other hand, sharing what you have with others is a moral good; it shows that you are acting on the right principle. The fact that you *can* share demonstrates that you actually have more than you need for yourself and family in the foreseeable future. But to have more than others and be unwilling to share is morally bad. (We shall see below how this value receives emphasis in the social relations of human beings.)

A moral disapproval of cruelty, it is interesting to discover, emerges from a consideration of the disease sanction in cases involving the relations between human and other-than-human

persons, as well as those between human beings. Cruelty to
animals, too, is subject to retribution. While it is necessary,
of course, for men to kill animals in order to live, what is
wrong is to cause them unnecessary suffering. I believe that
the disease sanction is applicable to the treatment of animals
because cruelty to individual animals is offensive to the "persons" who are their "masters." Thus, the breadth of the sanction against cruelty is as wide as it is deep in the Ojibwa
ethos.

A most conclusive demonstration of the wide range of the
sanction against cruelty is indicated by a case in which a boy
became ill because his father had caused a cannibal monster
unnecessary suffering. While all such cannibal monsters are
conceptualized as terrifying anthropomorphic beings, who
must be killed, some of them are human beings who have
turned into cannibals, and others are other-than-human persons, who lead an independent existence. To kill a [cannibal
monster] of the latter type is considered a feat of the utmost
heroism. It is a sure sign of greatness, because it is impossible
to accomplish it without the aid of powerful "helpers." Therefore, it was somewhat a surprise to me to discover that the
illness of the son of a [cannibal monster] slayer was attributed to the fact that his father had been cruel to one of these
cannibal monsters.

I was told about the case by Adam B., a doctor himself,
and the son of a doctor. He had accompanied his father when
the latter had been called in to treat Flatstone's, the slayer's,
son. When they arrived, the boy was spitting blood. "My
father talked for a little while. Then he took the rattle in
his hand and began to sing. While he was singing he suddenly
stopped. 'I can't go on,' he said. Then he tried again. After
singing some more he suddenly stopped again and said, 'I
don't think "my grandson" is going to get better. This blood
does not come from nothing. I guess it is your fault,' he said
to Flatstone. The latter did not reply. Then my father said,
'Do you remember that [cannibal monster] that overtook you
once when you were traveling?' 'Yes,' said Flatstone. 'What
did you do to him?' my father asked.

"Flatstone then told how he tried to hold the [cannibal
monster] down with his own strength, but failed. He then

called on one of his other-than-human helpers to come to his aid. The latter held him while Flatstone pulled out his hunting knife. He stabbed the [cannibal monster] in the back. 'I kept on stabbing him. The blood burst from his mouth. I kept at it. He did not last long after that. I killed him at last. But he suffered a long time before I killed him. He kept moving but I knew he was going to die.' My father said, 'Now you have told this, in two days your child will be better.' And the boy did get better," Adam B. added.

Adam B. also told me that it would have been all right if Flatstone had cut off the cannibal's head with an axe. What was wrong was the suffering caused, and the fact that in telling about his encounter, originally, Flatstone did not give a complete account: he was secretive about what had actually happened. It was also pointed out to me that Flatstone's daughter, who was an old woman at the time, spit up blood now and then.

Since power to cure illness that is a threat to health and life cannot be acquired by human beings solely through their own efforts, the ultimate validation of any kind of curing procedure is rooted in the interpersonal relations between a healer and other-than-human persons. And, just as the human recipient of the knowledge and power to cure has to fulfill obligations to "our grandfathers" in order to successfully practice his art, the human patient, in turn, cannot obtain a doctor's advice for nothing. The healer must be compensated for his services. Consequently, it is understandable why it is shocking to the Ojibwa when, occasionally, a healer, under the stress of illness himself, confesses that he never received any power from other-than-human sources. He reveals himself as a charlatan; he has been practicing medicine without a "license." Deception of this kind falls under the disease sanction. . . .

Viewed from the outside, [the disease sanction] has an equilibrating function: it reinforces the primary group organization of a hunting and gathering culture where no economic competition exists, where the circulation of goods does not depend upon a market, where there is a minimum of social stratification and no social machinery for adjudication of disputes, and where it is believed that whatever differences in power exist are due to other-than-human persons. What the disease sanction does is to support the independence and equality in status which individuals enjoy by discouraging deviations or innovations which would undermine and disrupt the Ojibwas' relatively simple form of social organization. . . .

Introduction to
Cultural Differences in Mental Disorders: An Italian and Irish Contrast in the Schizophrenias

This selection illustrates Benedict's point that the cultural context can provide fuller understanding of symptoms judged abnormal. Opler has related the differences in symptom frequencies to family dynamics, cultural values, and acceptable ways to express emotion within each culture. One might go further and notice how patterns of authority within the family reflect the political institutions of Ireland, under strong colonial rule, and Italy, which lacked strong centralized authority until fairly recently.

However, this study takes a very different view of mental illness than Benedict's. It assumes that schizophrenia is a disease entity which exists independently of cultural background, although patterned by it, and can therefore be compared from one group to another.

Using diagnostic categories such as schizophrenia without understanding the cultural background can distort the mental health worker's view of a patient. In some cultures, expecting a great deal of financial and emotional support from one's family may indicate self-confidence and strength rather than excessive dependency. Likewise, the connections between Catholicism and spiritualism in the Caribbean are widely held beliefs rather than individual ones. Understanding of cultural variables does not eliminate the need to know the individual patient, but can help to explain why his symptoms take the form they do.

The sample Opler studied was drawn from ethnic groups in New York City and included first, second, and third generation Irish and Italians. The homogeneity he found in symptoms, family dynamics, and values throughout all three generations suggests that these cultural patterns are resistant to the "melting pot." Care was taken to include patients for whom complete data was available; both psychiatric techniques and anthropological interviews were used in an effort to make the comparison between Irish and Italian patients rigorous and comprehensive.

---

12. CULTURAL DIFFERENCES IN MENTAL DISORDERS: AN ITALIAN AND IRISH CONTRAST IN SCHIZOPHRENIAS

by Marvin K. Opler

. . . In the matched samples of sixty patients, the mean age of Irish was 32 years as compared with the mean for Italians of 30.5. (Age limits for both groups were 18 to 45 at the beginning of the study, when the census was taken; it had shifted, of course, to 20 to 47 two years later when the study was completed.) For last grade of education, an Irish mean of 10.5 grades matched the Italian of 10.9. Intelligence potential, computed in Wechsler IQ averages and again by means, disclosed an Irish sample of 108.4 closely matching the Italian 105.5. Length of hospitalization was hardly different, with a mean for the first year of 1949.8 for Irish; and 1949.5 for Italian. In marital status, by actual count 25 Irish and 22 Italians were unmarried, although none of the remaining few marriages, when studied, could be counted distinct successes. Therefore, the variables matched or controlled for both samples were age, sex, educational level, intelligence, first year of hospitalization, marital status, absence of organic or

From *Culture and Mental Health*, The Macmillan Company, New York, 1959, pp. 425–42.

chronic conditions, and origin in the field study area. Only marital status showed, for Irish, a slight and possibly culturally influenced excess of celibacy. Yet illness and its particular pathology had made both groups primarily celibate, as we shall see.

Regional differences are important in Italian culture and less so among the Irish. As concerns this variable, we were again fortunate in eliminating it along with those just compared above. All Italians but one could trace ancestral lines from the extreme south of Italy (Naples southward) or from Sicily. Luckily, all Irish traced ancestry to "southwest" Irish counties and villages. The one lone North Italian who occurred in the census and came into the sample consequently proved to be an interesting exception to his group in both his psychodynamic and cultural patterns.

The tables given below summarize seven variables of a total of ten found to be significant in distinguishing Irish and Italian male schizophrenic patients. Earlier, at the outset of the research, we hypothesized these differences as accounting for two patterns, highly contrasting, in the etiology of each type of schizophrenia. We may begin by first explaining the differential terms used in accounting for each variable.

For reasons to be given below, we hypothesized that neither group would have a clearly male sexual identification in the illness state. Schizophrenics are notoriously troubled by homosexual strivings. However, it matters greatly in the total balance, or imbalance, of personality how such sexual strivings are shaped and whether they are latent or overt in character. Certainly, Italians stress even more forcefully than Irish the importance of masculinity for the male and femininity in females. However, they equally emphasize the expression of sexuality, as they do any human emotion or passion. In males who are schizophrenically ill and in whom both self-identity and sexual identification become impossible, the Italian model hypothesized was overt homosexuality, or a confused and active bisexuality which refused to pattern directly after the clearly male image of dominant and authoritarian fathers and elder brothers. Most of our Italian patients were, indeed, younger siblings who had moved quickly and impulsively, judging by their life histories, through a confused latent phase of sexual repulsion from a male role and into overt manifestations of homosexual behavior. The Irish, by contrast, both in our hypotheses and in fact, were fearful of a male role but repressive of homosexual trends based primarily on anxious attitudes toward mothers and other female images. One Irish patient who escaped this latent homosexual trend lost his mother at age three although he was still fearful of domineering women. Another solved the problem by attaching passively to a woman exactly twice his age whom he economically exploited in her confused senility. The vast majority of Irish male patients were latent homosexuals who avoided the female world, but repressed overt manifestations.

In keeping with these characteristics, the majority of Irish patients struggled with sin and guilt preoccupations concerning sexuality, whereas Italians had no sin or guilt preoccupations in this area. Instead, the Italian case histories and current ward behavior showed behavior disorders in the realm of poorly controlled impulses, weak personal attachments, and widely fluctuating or flighty emotional affects. The attitudes toward authority in the two groups diverged in parallel fashion, Italians having been verbally rejecting or actively flouting of authority in tests or case history, while Irish were hypothesized to be compliant for the most part, with only the most passive forms of outward resistance in evidence.

We hypothesized that the delusions, based on compensatory imagination in schizophrenics, would become fixed in Irish patients, and assume in them the typical paranoid forms of omnipotence or suspiciousness and persecution. While delusions are ordinarily developed in many forms of schizophrenia, it was hypothesized that, on the contrary, they would be largely absent among Italians, or if present would rarely be systematized or maintained with great fixity. Practically no Italians proved to have the highly systematized and elaborated delusions found frequently in the Irish patients, as we had hypothesized, so that the table below deals with the other factor of fixity. On the other hand, for reasons of clearer bodily emphasis, or in Schilder's phrase, "body image," we claimed Italian schizophrenics, male or female, would be given to hypochondriacal complaints and somatic or bodily preoccupations. As concerns alcoholism in case history, we ex-

pected to find this more frequently in Irish patients than in
the Italian. The tables given below summarize these seven
variables, which must then be considered in their meaningful
etiological sense.

	Irish	Italian	Total
Variable 1: Homosexual Types			
Latent	27	7	34
Overt	0	20	20
TOTAL	27	27	54
Variable 2: Sin and Guilt Preoccupations			
Present	28	9	37
Absent	2	21	23
TOTAL	30	30	60
Variable 3: Behavior Disorder			
Present	4	23	27
Absent	26	7	33
TOTAL	30	30	60
Variable 4: Attitude Towards Authority			
Compliant	24	9	33
Rejecting	6	21	27
TOTAL	30	30	60
Variable 5: Fixity in Delusional System			
No	7	20	27
Some	23	10	33
TOTAL	30	30	60
Variable 6: Somatic (Hypochondriacal) Complaints			
Present	13	21	34
Absent	17	9	26
TOTAL	30	30	60
Variable 7: Chronic Alcoholism			
Present	19	1	20
Absent	11	29	40
TOTAL	30	30	60

Statistical measures indicated that each of these variables
was highly significant in delineating differences between Irish
and Italian schizophrenics.

Having just indicated a skeletonized set of differences between our two samples, it remains to account for the development of each kind of pathology. The previous community sur-
veys in New York City contained for each ethnic group a

whole continuum of persons and families whose behavior ranged from normative or "normal" standards of conduct to those who were aberrant or deviant. Having studied well or moderately ill Irish and Italians in their family settings and community groups, one could distinguish for each group its distinctive cultural contributions and backgrounds, its particular pace of cultural change, and its typical or special patterns of stress in family conflicts. Each group, Irish, Italian, Puerto Rican, or others, sanctioned or interdicted outlets for emotional expression. In the range of persons and families from the healthy and well-balanced to those evidencing pathology, the cultural patterns even where undergoing change provided the necessary framework for understanding the meanings of emotional stress and conflict, both in the pathogenic families and individuals and in those who seemed to be presumably symptom free. The crucial point for each cultural group of the eight studied was that it was the normative side of the continuum, the ongoing ethnic group, which helped define the kinds of conflict or repression, the types of emotional expression, the system of values, or the functioning of the family for each individual. While Freud had stated long ago that neurosis is the price paid for civilization, instead we found that each culture or subculture contained its designs for living. In each, consequently, there were various stresses and strains, and well-functioning families as well as pathogenic ones. Creative and negative features typified the genius and the pitfalls of each cultural system. As a result, we conducted no search for a single etiology of mental illnesses such as characterized the nineteenth century, but instead insisted upon viewing each family and each patient in his meaningful cultural setting.

Therefore, three variables not included in the above tables were considered of primary significance. All were prior in effect or earlier acting than those already listed. The first, which we shall call Variable A, dealt with the possibilities in each cultural group, by virtue of its family system, for the development of negative and destructive emotions of various sorts. While it is true that in schizophrenias elements of hostility and anxiety may coexist in different degrees, the amount of each emotion in such admixtures and the means by which it is expressed or controlled is the really crucial matter. D. H. Funkenstein's contrast between anxiety states premised on fear and those based upon hate is relevant here. We added that this dichotomy in the schizophrenias (fear versus hate) be taken together with Freudian considerations as to whether these emotions were expressed or denied outlet in typical family structures of a given cultural group. We noted that in Irish families, particularly those poorly organized, the central figure is usually the mother. Her authority extends to all matters of household management, including not only child-rearing but the major decisions governing the home. She achieves this status by reason of her matronage and not infrequently conceives of the distaff as the symbol of authority, of family domain, and of emotional control. Historically, Irish fathers of the southwest counties were frequently in straitened economic circumstances, and were shadowy and ineffectual figures in the home. It was hypothesized, on the basis of this type of family structure, that anxiety, tinged with fear and hate, would be the resultant emotion in Irish male patients who as sons had been raised to view themselves as "forever boys and burdens." In two-thirds of the Irish cases, this primary anxiety (with some hostility usually compressed by fear) was directed toward all female figures. In only three cases of a total forty did the father appear more centrally, and in these the entire pattern of illness shifted to the "Italian model" in most details. In one of these, as stated above, the mother had died when the patient was three years of age.

In sharp contrast, Italian cultural values set greater store on male parental or eldest sibling dominance while at the same time reinforcing more direct expressions of the resultant hostile emotions. This acting-out of feelings brought more hostility to the fore in poorly repressed conflicts with fathers or elder male siblings. One Italian patient, for example, entered the acute phase of illness at the time of his elder brother's wedding and expressed himself, with floridly violent accusations, against his father. In practically all cases there was a strong repulsion from the father, elder brother, and even surrogate authority figures. The Italian mothers, in such instances, were often subtly rejecting and preferred the oldest son. In some cases, the mother, playing a subordinate role in the family, had compensated by assuming a mildly seductive and pampering role in relationships with the son. One could trace the effects of a harsh and punitive or domineering father. The mother compensated for her own feelings of neglect at the father's hands by building up hostile forms of impulsiveness in these sons, along with features of poor emotional control. Italian patients, even when labeled like Irish as schizophrenics with paranoid reaction, had more prominent problems of emotional overflow (schizo-affective features) which took the form of elated overtalkativeness, curious mannerisms, grinning and laughing hyperactivity, or even assaultiveness. Even hostility directed toward oneself came into evidence when elated excitements gave way to inept suicidal attempts. One-third of the Italian sample showed such periodic excitements with confusion and emotional lability (catatonic excitements) while the other two-thirds were subject to extreme mood swings in which the depressed and quiescent periods gave way to destructive outbursts, elation, suicidal behavior, or curious mannerisms. In brief, all Italian patients had so much affective coloring, aimed primarily at male figures and images, that the paranoid schizophrenic label seemed to fit them poorly.

A second primary difference in the samples, which we shall call Variable B, dealt with the central tendencies in each culture for channeling emotional expression. To some extent, this expression of the emotional life in each ethnic group applied also to female patients. Italian culture generally sanctions the freer expression of emotions, and emotion may be expressed, in lower class groups particularly, in bodily action. The Irish, on the contrary, are famous for a greater constriction of activity and their most endearing trait, which no doubt compensates for this constriction, is an equally rich fantasy life. In Freudian theory, fantasy may substitute, almost vicariously, for action. We have, indeed, already noted the intensity of emotion and its expression in activity in poorly controlled Italian patients. The counterpart in the Irish sample of patients was a fantasy substitute for action. While Italian patients might oscillate between hyperactivity and underactivity, or show an inability to time their activities, thoughts, or emotions effectively, the Irish, with no such difficulties in estimating time or guarding their emotions, showed an inversely large proportion of rich and extensive fantasy. Their more deeply repressed conflicts consequently took a more delusional and paranoid form. One Irishman, for example, repeatedly gave for two years a most lurid series of accounts of the death of each family member, blaming his mother for a horrible accident which befell the father. The father had died at a ripe old age in a hospital of a common ailment. With each monotonous recital, the father's death in front of the home became more blood-stained and painful. The mother became a cold, emotionless, and witchlike figure described in an affect-less tone and cursed in a magical, ritual manner.

Linked with these two primary variables of family authority structure and the channeling of emotional expression were other cultural variables affecting the emotional life. With Italian males, more direct feelings of hostility flooded up from shallowly repressed levels, connected with feelings of repulsion from a father, elder brother, or surrogate authority figures. As concerns sexual identification (Variable 1 of tables), two-thirds of the Italian sample showed active homosexual tend-encies which had at one time or another been overtly prac-ticed. This rejection of a male identity and strong repulsion from male role fitted the variables already considered—hatred of the father, lack of stability in the mother, and the cultural sanctions for expression of emotion. Impulsiveness, acting-out, and the emotional overflow might be expected among the ill of this cultural group. This acting-out of impulse was often noted in a background of sociopathic escapades common in childhood or in youth. For the same variables, the Irish male patient, beset with anxiety and fear of female figures early in life, likewise lacked possibilities of a firm male identifica-tion, but here the fear was centered on the opposite sex, and the sexual repressions and sin or guilt emphases of the culture made for a repressive, latent form of homosexuality. Instead of the open refusal to be male, or repulsion from male role as in Italian patients (nonidentification in Italians), the Irish had instead a fearful or anxious lack of positive male identi-fication. Here the latent homosexual tendency was controlled by added distortions and repressions. If repressed sufficiently, the Irish patient was pallidly asexual. Only three, as the tables

indicate, managed to achieve or maintain the asexual balance
in repression. Of twenty-seven who were latent homosexuals,
the distortions of body image had occurred already in some
who had bizarre delusional misidentifications as to their sexual
characteristics. One such delusional form may serve to illustrate the patient who believed his entire bodily structure in
the front was covered by an "apron"; this apron had certain
feminine characteristics, like periodic bleeding or the capacity
to distract the patient's thoughts ("affecting my thoughts,"
adversely, of course).

Beyond family structure, type of sexual identification problem, and the channels for emotional expression in each culture lie a further series of consequences for emotional stress
and its pitfalls in poorly organized families. The sexual misidentifications (in Irish males) and nonidentifications (or
refusals to identify properly in the Italian series) are contrasting types which occur in quite different defensive emotional
structures. In this sense, Variables 2 and 3 of tables may be
considered concomitant variations or further consequences on
the basic themes of stress problems in family structure and
affective controls. Obviously, personality traits exist and function together in the total business of living. Thus the concepts
of sin and guilt, particularly in the sexual area, were built
up in the Irish patients and were readily accessible in their
cultural stock-in-trade. Not only did twenty-eight Irish patients torment and exacerbate themselves with such sin and
guilt formulae, but twenty-one Italians of similar faith did
not apply sin and guilt irritations to their sexual ideologies.
Again, with the Irish, such formulae often became delusional
and persecutory. A particular kind of mythology, prominent
among nonliterate peoples, and concerning a toothed, castrat-
ing vagina, occurred in the setting of incestuous guilts about
feelings toward sisters and other female relatives in several
Irish cases. Contrary to this, twenty-six Irish patients showed
no evidence in the hospital or in life history of having been
involved in any sociopathic behavior, whereas twenty-three
Italians showed repeated and marked evidence of behavior
disorders. As we have seen, the attitude toward authority
(Variable 4 of tables), more consciously expressed in instru-
ments like Sentence Completions or exemplified in life

histories and ward behavior, indicated a similar difference in attitude, with twenty-four compliant Irish patients to almost the same number of more rebellious Italians.

Variable 5 of tables explored the prediction that the Irish patients, with their anxious fantasies, their latent and repressed homosexual trends, and the indoctrinated "sex-is-sin" feelings of guilt would be forced to build fixed delusional systems. While Irish patients used this delusional or fantasy defense against their sexual misidentification problems and shattered self-esteem, the Italians mainly expressed their sense of defeat and hostility in mood swings, excitements, and impulsive behavior. Thus delusional fixity occurred in a ratio greater than three to one for Irish, while exactly two-thirds of the Italian patients had no delusions manifest during the study, and half the remaining ten had only changeable and minor delusional episodes. On the other hand, as might be expected, the Italian patients distinctly led in Variable 6 of the tables, in the frequency with which hypochondriacal complaints about imagined somatic disorders were mentioned. For Variable 7 of the tables, only one of the Italian patients had ever been chronically addicted to alcohol although every individual liked wines, whiskey, or beer. In the Irish, on the contrary, almost two-thirds had sought an escape from problems in protracted periods of alcohol addiction.

In discussing this relationship between environment and mental illnesses, such authors as Stanton and Schwartz in their book *The Mental Hospital* or Fromm-Reichmann in her *Principles of Intensive Psychotherapy* have discussed patients' reactions to ways of handling them, to interaction processes on the ward, or to different psychotherapeutic approaches. These authors concede a general validity to the idea that no patients, not even schizophrenics, live in a cultural vacuum. But neglected in the literature is the related thought that the course of illness and the very structuring of personality bear a cultural imprint. All nine variables discussed thus far show an inner consistency and integration of defenses which constitute two separate kinds of illness. Psychiatrists in treating *each* type can be more effective if they understand these linkages of culture and personality. What Sullivan called "the schizophrenic ways of life" can be

related and regeared to more positive cultural determinants
only after we understand the differences in family structures,
in self-identification problems, and in methods of emotional
control which have made up the characteristic blend in any
balance of defenses.

A final or tenth variable was therefore used in the study
to describe this balance of defenses. We found it favoring
fantasy and withdrawal patterns for the Irish to the extent
of paranoid reactions. The Italian patients suffered from disorders of poor emotional and impulse control. The Irish were
most anxious in relations with persons of opposite sex and
the shaping of basic personality contained notions of male
inadequacy, fear of females, and latent homosexual tendencies
intensified by sin and guilt preoccupations. With the Irish,
self-esteem and identification were destroyed together, and
weakness, inadequacy feelings, suspiciousness, and paranoid
delusions had taken over. Hence the bodily somatizations and
hypochondriacal complaints, common in Italians, were rare
in the Irish. Delusions became fixed in paranoid channels,
and fantasy and distortion were used to preserve the system
intact. These were the quiet, anxious men, fearful of anything
which might separate them from the protection of the ward
and their well-regulated delusional systems.

Obviously, the Italian patients were different not only on
each count, but in the total pattern of symptoms. As such,
they represented other problems in management and therapy.
A family structure, diametrically different from the Irish,
favored overt expression of homosexuality. The different cultural emphasis on emotional expression led to the acting-out
of impulse. The strength of anger in this emotional lability,
the motor excitements, or flaring-up of affect could now throw
the patient into confusional affective states, or into the excitements, periodic and sometimes destructive, which characterized an even greater proportion. This balance, or typical reso-
lution of defenses, was most important in the actual handling
and maintenance of rapport with each patient. . . .

Introduction to
Indigenous Yoruba Psychiatry

Just as psychological symptoms have to be understood in the context of the culture in which they develop, so must psychotherapeutic techniques be attuned to the culture in which the patient is to function. Other cultures, such as the Yoruba of Nigeria, can offer insights that will be useful in making treatment in Western societies more appropriate.

Hospitalization does not remove the patient from his family or community among the Yoruba. While patients reside in treatment centers, family and friends help them back to recovery by nursing, feeding them and being involved in the treatment process. As the patient recovers, he is integrated into the community through work and participation in the healer's household, which serves as a kind of day hospital. The patient is not dehumanized by his treatment, because the healer in the Yoruba treatment center handles his professional distance very differently from most Western practitioners.

The discharge ceremony marks an important change in social status from sickness to health, which is not ritualized in Western societies. The Yoruba recognize recovery, which allows other people to regard the patient as normal. In our culture the stigma which follows the former patient often prevents people from trusting him and treating him as normal.

The joining of an Orisa cult gives the discharged patient the support vital to resuming his life. The Orisas are deities surrounded by esoteric lore and secrecy, and the initiation into this group gives him a new identity which is approved of by his community. He gains a new circle of friends from whom he can draw support. This kind of aftercare succeeds where Western aftercare may fail because it is integrated into values

held by patient, family, and community, while Western hospitals and clinics are often feared because they are alien to
the patient's world. Although the Yoruba healer is a private
practitioner, the kind of treatment described by Prince is
community-based.

---

13. INDIGENOUS YORUBA PSYCHIATRY
by Raymond Prince

. . . The Yoruba language contains a number of expressions
for psychiatric disturbances. Many are used rather loosely by
the healers, as well as by the general populace. Indeed the
affixing of labels does not seem to assume much importance
in the healers' minds. The following labels, however, seem
to be used more or less consistently in the area studied.

THE PSYCHOSES

By far the commonest diagnostic label applied at native
treatment centers was *Were*. It typically refers to a chronic
psychotic who is careless in dress and vagrant, talks irrationally, and suffers auditory or visual hallucinations. The patient's harmlessness is generally stressed. Sometimes the term
is applied to more acute psychoses. Many chronic and perhaps
acute schizophrenics would be included in this category.

Asinwin is usually applied to an acute psychotic episode
with sudden onset. Several informants emphasized that this
kind of psychosis is the most dangerous, for the patient is
more liable to commit suicide or homicide during this illness

Adapted from *Magic, Faith and Healing*, edited by Ari Kiev, The
Free Press, New York, 1964, pp. 84–119.

than during any other. The Western counterpart would be
an acute schizophrenic episode, mania, catatonic excitement,
or agitated delirium.

Dindinrin refers to a withdrawn, suspicious, and uncom-
municative psychotic of a chronic schizophrenic type. Some
healers say that *asinwin* might become *were* and that both
were and *asinwin* might become *dindinrin* if they are not
properly treated.

Danidani (*edani*) refers to either a severely regressed psychotic or a mental defective. None of the patients I observed
at treatment centers was so labeled.

Were alaso (*were* that wears clothes) refers to a psychotic
with a well preserved personality. "You may see him on the
street and not realize he is mad. He is dressed properly and
may speak sensibly at times, but he is still mad all the same."

Were agba denotes psychosis associated with old age.

Abisinwin is postpartum psychosis. "It generally starts
about three days after delivery; I had one last year, and she
strangled her child. It lasted three months. All such patients
should have their children removed from them."

Were d'ile (*were* of the lineage) is, as it implies, hereditary
psychosis.

THE PSYCHONEUROSES

Yoruba healers often do not make a clear distinction between physical disease and the psychoneuroses. This failure
is understandable because many Yoruba neuroses present
largely physical symptoms. The following diagnoses are commonly used and seem to refer to psychoneuroses, although
they may include deficiencies and other organic ills in some
cases.

Ori ode (hunter's head) is a designation that covers one
of the commonest neuroses suffered by the Yoruba. The patient has somatic complaints of burning, crawling, or thump-
ing in his head, which often spreads through the whole body.
Visual symptoms like dimness of vision and "dazzling" of the
eyes are common. Insomnia, dizziness, and trembling may occur. Several informants say that the patient may become psy-

chotic if the *ori ode* becomes too intense. There are several native descriptions of the condition:

> It is like an insect in the forehead; it starts in the nose and gets to the head; it knocks his brain and works through his whole body. His eyes will be no good; he can't see anything and his ears will be buzzing—it is a kind of mental trouble. . . .
>
> Something will be striking in the brain as if to say a blacksmith is striking an anvil. He will be hearing a buzzing in the ears but no voices. There is burning in the head, and weakness. If it becomes too much, it may cover the eyes and the patient can't see, or sometimes the head is turned and the man runs mad . . .

Inarun, a condition "which comes from God," has as its common symptoms weakness, burning of the body or itching, skin rashes, dimness of vision, impotence or "black menstruation," deadness of the feet, paralysis of the legs, and occasionally organic psychosis: "Tired and weak, body scratching him, impotent, he feels hot on his body and might get paralyzed legs and may go mad; talking irrationally, he may look at an object for hours. He has memory loss and may cry a lot."

Aluro, *egba*, and *ategun* seem to cover both organic and hysterical paralyses, which were not clearly distinguished by my informants.

Gbohungbohun refers to hysterical aphonia.

Afota is a type of hysterical blindness.

Aiyiperi is a complex concept that includes hysterical convulsive disorders, posturings, and tics, as well as psychomotor seizures and probably tetanus. Some healers also include *warapa* (*grand mal* epilepsy) and *giri* (convulsions in children) under this designation.

Ipa were is madness associated with epilepsy.

In the cases I studied at the native treatment centers, there were fifty cases of *were*, thirteen cases of *dindinrin*, five cases of *asinwin*, four cases of *were alaso*, four cases of *were d'ile*, four cases of *ori ode*, two cases of *ipa were*, one case of *warapa*, one case of *inarun*, nine in a general category of other, and eight cases undiagnosed. . . .

THE TREATMENT CENTERS

In a secluded section of the town of Abeokuta stands a typical treatment center, that of Mr. F. His house is a one-story, L-shaped mud structure with a tin roof, set in a grove of palms. There are perhaps ten rooms, spacious, cool, and, apart from a few low stools, without furniture. The house is always a hive of activity, with his patients and his numerous wives and children cooking and eating, pounding *garri*, feeding babies, grinding medicines, and peeling kola nuts. Relatives of resident patients, friends, and outpatients are continually coming and going. Behind the house are two smaller buildings, one housing patients and the other a kind of "pharmacy" with three open fires and numerous pots for the preparation of medicines.

The hut for the patients is divided in two for male and female patients; in each section are two "seclusion" rooms with iron bars on the windows and chains hanging from the ceiling to put around the necks of disturbed patients. These rooms are also unfurnished; the mud floors are covered with grass mats. Behind the patients' hut there is a large grove of coconut palms. It is cool and pleasant there, but I have seldom seen it used by the patients, who seem to find the bustle of the big house more to their taste. The hut can accommodate eight to ten patients, and others may be given quarters in the main house. Psychotic patients (and the great majority of patients who "live in" are psychotic) are generally shackled for the first few days or weeks until they can be trusted not to abscond. The average length of stay in this center is from three to four months.

Growing around the patients' hut and also in a fenced-off garden nearby are many of the trees and herbs that are used in therapy *odundun, rinrin, ekan-ekun, ajeofole, agunmona, apikan, asofeyeje,* and many others.

The following extract from my notes illustrates something of the nature of the patient population at this center at the time of one visit:

August 2nd, 1961, 5 p.m.—F. was very busy and there were several people sitting outside who had been waiting to see

him since the early afternoon. On my arrival F. was dis-
puting with a patient's parents over the amount of money
for food for their son. . . . There were ten patients "living
in": One woman was living in the main house and was suffering from *ori ode* [psychoneurosis]. . . . Three women
shackled in the patients' hut were suffering from psychoses
due to *epe* [curse]; one of these was heavily sedated with
asofeyeje, snoring loudly and stretched out on the floor.
. . . He had also two new young boys with *warapa* [grand
mal epilepsy]; he said that before they came they had two
or three seizures a day, but now they had been free of seizures for several days. . . . There was one chronic elderly
female there whom I had seen on several occasions before;
she was sitting gloomily alone on a bench before the hut.
Her illness is due to her failure to worship Obatala [one of
the *Orisas*]; her relatives are Christian, and they refuse to
pay for a sacrifice to Obatala and F. believes she will not
recover until this is done. . . . There is also a psychotic
girl from Ghana; F. says they do not know about *Rauwolfia*
in Ghana. . . . Two partially recovered male patients were
out on errands for F. and I did not see them . . .

Seven of the sixteen healers did not have separate buildings for their patients but used certain rooms within their
own houses and did not have the spacious grounds enjoyed
by Mr. F.'s patients.

THERAPY AT TREATMENT CENTERS

A psychotic patient is usually brought to the treatment
center by a throng of relatives or by the healer, who, using his
magical powers, may have captured the patient. If he is ex-
cited, he is bound or shackled. He may then be cooled down
by a wash with snail's water, a clear, cool watery fluid found
in the cone of the giant land snail. The patient may be
stripped and his head shaved and rubbed with this fluid. He
is then given a potion, usually containing *asofeyeje* root
(*Rauwolfia*), and he goes to sleep. Some healers give a
purgative-emetic mixture to "weaken" the patient before giving the sedative or tranquilizing agent.

Generally speaking, each healer has his own standard approach to treating patients, and it is only when he sees that

the patient is not responding that he changes his medicine. He sometimes decides on the cause in this way; that is, he gives the patient *epe* (curse) medicine, and, if that does not cause improvement, he decides that it is Sopono's work and applies *ero Sopono*. Alternatively, he uses divination or consults with the witches if the patient is not doing well.

Some healers routinely carry out blood sacrifices at admission. Such a sacrifice may be a sheep, goat, or fowl and is aimed at appeasing the witches or spirits involved. In cases where *epe* (curse) or *asasi* (sorcery) is the cause of the trouble, a detoxifying procedure is carried out—medicine is introduced into the blood through razor cuts in the scalp, a procedure that will be enlarged upon later.

Treatment with tranquilizing and other herbal medicines (generously laced with magic) usually continues for three or four months. Doses are given daily or every two days.

As the patient improves, the shackles are removed, and he is given the run of the treatment center and the healer's house. He may work on the healer's farm or hire out as casual labor to other farmers. He may be allowed to go to market or run errands for the healer. Most healers require that a relative of the patient stay at the treatment center, especially during the early period. Relatives provide nursing care and feed the patient.

When the patient is ready to return home, a discharge ceremony, aimed at preventing a recurrence of his psychosis, is held for him. This ritual includes a blood sacrifice and is often performed beside a river. Some of the ceremonies are quite elaborate and expensive; they symbolize final cleansing of the illness and sometimes "death and rebirth" into a new life.

Charges for treatment vary from twenty to seventy pounds —at least, that is what the healers claim; how much they do actually receive is hard to say. One of their favorite topics of conversation, however, is the perfidy of relatives who do not pay their fees. They also emphasize that, if they are properly paid, they can do a much more rapid and complete healing job. These healers certainly do not suffer from "therapeutic nihilism," and almost all were most emphatic about their ability to cure all illness—"If there is money!" . . .

Discharge Ceremonies. As in the West, Yoruba psychiatric patients suffer frequent relapses. Many of the patients studied at the treatment centers had previously received treatment in one or more other centers (including Aro, Lantoro, and Yaba Hospitals, the Western-style psychiatric hospitals in the Region). The healers usually attributed these relapses to inadequate previous treatment because of relatives who were not able to pay the required money. This high rate of relapse is reflected in the healers' preoccupation with discharge ceremonies. These ceremonies take highly diverse forms, depending upon the healer and upon the cause of the illness. The common feature is the sacrifice of an animal or bird accompanied by incantations to assure that the illness will never return.

I observed the following ceremony at Ife. It was performed for a young woman who had just recovered from a psychotic episode. It took place in a secluded part of a river about five miles from the town. On the river bank, the patient put off her clothes and dressed in a new white wrapper. The healer, his assistant, carrying three white doves, and the patient waded into midstream where the waist-high water flowed swiftly. The patient's head was shaved. The healer placed a piece of soap on the breast of one of the doves. Using it as a living sponge, he dipped it into the water and lathered the patient's head and body. The body of the drowned dove was thrown downstream. The second dove was decapitated, and its blood was spattered over the patient's head and smeared over the upper part of her body. Again she was washed and the dove flung downstream. A cross of razor cuts was made over her scalp, and into the cuts was rubbed a mixture of blessed camwood, chalk, and the blood of doves (which had been prepared previously). The patient was divested of her white wrapper, which floated away downstream. Ashore, her body and head were again generously rubbed with camwood and chalk, the last dove was decapitated, and the blood again spattered over her body. She then stood on the body of the dead bird, incantations were recited, the bird's body was flung into the river, and the ceremony was complete.

After her return to the doctor's house, another dove was sacrificed and its blood sprinkled over the threshold. Palm oil was poured up the steps, over the threshold, and into the house. The patient could then enter. . . .

The symbolism of the ceremony is partially apparent. Doves are symbols of peace, their blood mingled with that of the patient brings tranquillity. The evil, which is partly present in the patient's blood and partly a kind of coating over her head and body, is borne away on the bodies of the doves and the white cloth (anyone picking up the doves or the cloth will contract the illness). Some elements suggest death and rebirth—wrapping in white cloth, the use of the camwood and chalk, the spattering with blood are all features of Yoruba burial ritual. At any rate, the ceremony is clearly a "rite de passage" from the sick mode to the healthy mode. . . .

Introduction to
The Effects of Consumer Control on the Delivery of Services

Yoruba treatment centers contain many of the elements the Hill-West Haven community mental health centers are striving for: the agency is responsive to community needs, there is personalized contact with a staff made up of people similar enough to community members to understand them. Even though the purposes are similar, this selection illustrates how the way of achieving them in a Western urban setting has to be very different because well-established bureaucratic patterns must be changed. That the staff of mental health centers has to consult with community spokesmen in order to set up collaborative boards suggests how out of touch the mental health apparatus has become.

The community mental health movement is imposed from the top—federally sponsored, not dependent on the community for funding, and internally controlled. Transition to community controls means a change from regarding the consumer as passive to regarding him as an active participant. This change has implications for how the staff and clients view each other: the staff must learn to respect patients as knowing priorities, even though they may lack expertise in implementing them. Decision thus becomes a collaborative process rather than one-sided. Members of the staff find themselves in a much more challenging position, subject to evaluation by the clients and by each other. Tischler's use of diagnostic categories to describe staff reaction is an example of this changed position.

Both the methods and goals of community control are closely related to anthropological models. Participant observation is one way the mental health workers in Hill-West Haven gained insights into the community. In non-Western societies, there is very little separation between an institution and the people it serves. Where this separation has developed to a very high degree in a complex society, joint responsibility for achieving mutual goals can minimize bureaucratic distance.

14. THE EFFECTS OF CONSUMER CONTROL ON THE DELIVERY OF SERVICES

by Gary L. Tischler, M.D.

The past decade has witnessed the coalescence of a political movement advocating the decentralization of authority with a social movement founded upon the belief that health is a right of the many and not a privilege of the few. In urban areas, the coalescence of the health rights movement and the political quest for the decentralization of authority has generated increased pressure for community control over human services. Traditionally, health care systems claim for themselves the prerogative of defining service priorities and reviewing ongoing program. The rationale for internal control and accountability is that: (1) system overload is prevented through keeping service commitments within reasonable bounds; (2) personnel are buffered from extraneous outside interference as they work at their allocated tasks; and (3) adequate quality control of ongoing service is assured.

Institutional self-definition, however, tends to become an unfortunate corollary of internal control and accountability. In the mental health field, institutional self-definition has allowed health care systems to limit their psycho-social problem solving to those areas that they deem of primary import. As a result, service gaps were created that led to massive dis-

From American Journal of Orthopsychiatry, Volume 41, No. 3, April 1971, pp. 501–5.

crimination against the more disadvantaged sectors of the population and contributed to a growing estrangement between service institutions and their clients. Recent crises at the New Jersey College of Medicine and Lincoln Hospital testify not only to the affinity between the issues of health rights and community power, but also to the need for developing workable and effective models of creative collaboration between provider and consumer. Over the past four years, the Hill-West Haven Division of the Connecticut Mental Health Center has been striving to elaborate such a model.

THE HILL-WEST HAVEN DIVISION

The Hill-West Haven Division is an integral part of the Connecticut Mental Health Center. A collaborative effort of the State of Connecticut and Yale University, the Center was organized along the lines of a unit system in order to facilitate the testing out of divergent models of care. One of its original units was the Hill-West Haven Division. Supported by a Community Mental Health Center Staffing Grant, the Division is the only component of the Center that serves the population of a geographically defined catchment area.

The catchment consists of approximately 75,000 people and includes the Hill neighborhood of New Haven and the City of West Haven. West Haven is a predominantly white, lower-middle-class working town, heavily dependent upon New Haven based agencies for social and health care services. The Hill, the last major inner city area to undergo urban redevelopment, is currently in the throes of marked social transition. Poor income, unemployment, low educational level, substandard housing, and overcrowding characterize the neighborhood.

From its inception, the Hill-West Haven Division was charged with the responsibility for providing comprehensive mental health services to the catchment. In meeting that charge, a service model was designed that would not only accommodate the essential elements of comprehensive care defined in the Community Mental Health Center Act of 1963, but also allow for the development of a preventive focus aimed at modifying features of the social, economic, and institutional environment that breed alienation, apathy, regression, and powerlessness.

The model holds that *service to a community* represents a *working alliance between consumer and provider* (1) to seek out and modify vectors within a community harmful to mental health through research, indirect clinical service, and social action; (2) to support individuals in their efforts at dealing with life stresses, whether they be internal or external, through the provision of a full complement of direct clinical services that assure ease of access and continuity of care to catchment residents; and (3) to develop an effective manpower base within the community with skills essential for carrying out the above tasks through a training program for community residents. Consumer participation, social action, direct and indirect clinical care, research, and training are each viewed as critical dimensions of service to a community.

CONSUMER PARTICIPATION

Consumer participation forms the core of the service model outlined above. The Division began with the premise that a consumer—wise in the ways of his own world, aware of the complex problems inherent in negotiating a service maze, and knowledgeable about the impact of that maze upon both his life space and survival capacity—has the experience, right, and obligation to participate in ordering the service patterns for his community.

The next step involved translating that premise into reality through verifying the consumer's role as a collaborator-in-service rather than just a recipient-of-service. Verification required building regulatory mechanisms into the system that guaranteed the sharing of responsibility and authority. The existence of such mechanisms not only confirmed the alliance between the consumer and the provider, it also created a set of checks and balances within the system to control the subsequent emergence of major service gaps.

FROM PARTICIPATION TO REGULATION

Initially, citizen involvement with the Hill-West Haven

Division was informal. While counsel was sought from the community around issues of program, goals, and policy, while involvement with numerous grass roots groups characterized the Division's early functioning, the prerogatives of the community and the exact nature of its authority were never clearly spelled out. This was in large measure due to the amorphousness and fractionalism of the catchment communities. No mechanisms or structures existed in either community for the coordination or regulation of health and social services. As a result, a major portion of the Division's initial activity was devoted to community development. This activity was undertaken with community groups and other agencies. The problems encountered and the vicissitudes in community relations that followed represent a separate subject in and of itself. Over a three-year period, however, organizational structures did emerge within the Hill and West Haven capable of representing the health and social service interests of their communities.

In the spring of 1969, consumer involvement in the regulation of the Hill-West Haven Division was formalized. Each community designated a Consumer Board to which the Division was to be accountable. These Boards had wide responsibilities in the areas of program development, personnel practices, and the establishment of service and research priorities. All subsequent changes in the basic structure and direction of the Division were to be approved by the Boards, which could also act as initiators of change.

EFFECTS ON THE DELIVERY OF SERVICE

The impact upon the Hill-West Haven Division of the shift from informal community participation to more formal consumer control can be measured in both structural and functional terms. The former involves questions of organization and program; the latter, questions of task performance.

Structurally, the effect of the transition has been minimal. That is to say, the Division is organized as it was and offers essentially the same services today as it did previously. In West Haven, the Board has given priority to the care of children and the elderly. Staff allocation and program planning are now being reoriented to meet that priority. In the Hill, the major emphasis to date has been upon personnel and personnel practices. Staffing patterns have been modified to include more community residents among the work force. A training program geared to sensitizing all staff to the life style and needs of the poor has been advocated. Programmatically, concern has been expressed about the current allocation of resources for dealing with the problem of drug addiction.

Functionally, the transition was accompanied by modifications in staff task performance. Since staff act as mediators between a health care system and its consumers, the manner in which they respond to an organizational shift can affect the delivery of service. Four basic patterns of staff response were noted at the time of the transition. These included:

1. FEAR AND DISORGANIZATION

This response pattern was characterized by a belief in consumer irrationality and the certainty that the care-giving agent would be turned upon and struck down in some act of retribution. For these people, consumer regulation was equivalent to mass anarchy. They reacted as though things were out of control and felt that the support upon which they had previously relied was no longer available. Rumors proliferated about rape and theft in the parking lot. Concern with assaultive behavior preoccupied inpatient staff. Racial and sexual imagery permeated all conversations.

2. RETRENCHMENT AND DENIAL

This response pattern was typified by an attitude of provider-power and the certainty that the "tried and true" would prevail. For these people, consumer control was an inconvenience. They firmly believed that no change in the status quo was possible. On the inpatient service, control and orderliness were the topics of the day. Disaffection with leadership was expressed for having failed to educate the community sufficiently as to how things really were in the mental health field. It was generally felt that had the community known, they would never have wanted to get involved.

3. ROMANCE AND SURRENDER

This response was characterized by reverence and awe of consumer expertise. For these people, consumer regulation was seen as an opportunity, but an opportunity that could only be seized if they were to surrender all of what they had been. *Black Rage, The Autobiography of Malcolm X*, and *Soul on Ice* were discussed with an enchantment previously reserved for Hildegard Peplau, Sigmund Freud, Carl Rogers, Gerald Caplan, and Harris Peck. After all the years of sailing in uncharted seas with captains who knew little of navigation, the opportunity was at hand to achieve knowledge and relevance in one fell swoop.

4. COLLABORATIVE ENGAGEMENT

This response pattern was most common. It was characterized by an acceptance of the consumer as a bona fide collaborator tempered by anticipatory anxiety. The anxiety stemmed from the uncertainty of whether the Boards, in the process of ordering service patterns and establishing priorities for communities, might begin to prescribe treatment for individuals. For these people, consumer control was seen as a vehicle for facilitating creative innovation following community dialogue. Latent concern existed that a reordering of service priorities might well order some staff members right out of jobs. Overall, however, the group's reaction was positive, although tentative. They reserved the right to judge the outcome on the basis of their own experience.

Of the response patterns noted above, all but the last tended to compromise the staff's capacity to perform their assigned roles and, therefore, had an adverse effect upon the delivery of service. In the first instance, anxiety was so great that it led to a functional paralysis and abrogation of responsibility that was catastrophic; in the second, retrenchment was followed by a constriction and rigidity that diminished spontaneity and flexibility and resulted in an impaired capacity to listen or to hear; and, in the third instance, a dilletantism developed characterized by the absence of a clear conceptual focus around which work could be oriented and an inconsistent, tentative approach to problem solving with clients. These three response patterns either proved transient and gave way to collaborative engagement or were so discomfiting that the staff member felt compelled to leave the Division. Periodically, during times of stress within the Division or strain between the Division and the community, the reaction patterns re-emerge; however, they are less intense and involve fewer people.

CONCLUSIONS

These are troubled times for mental health professionals. A confluence of social, political, and historical forces has stripped the mystique away from the clinician-healer. In the process, the exact limits of responsibility that had been accepted for dealing with the mental health problems of our society were laid bare. These limits proved unacceptable. Change was demanded. The gauntlet of comprehensive care was cast down. As the clinician-healer stooped to pick it up, the armor in which he had encased himself creaked, thus confirming the need for change. Change has been difficult, however, particularly since it is perceived as being imposed, involves theoretical and practical issues that are far from resolved, and requires individuals to enter realms where they had never dreamt to tread.

In the preceding pages, the attempt of one health care system to come to terms with the call for change was outlined, the rationale for a shift from institutional to consumer control set forth, and the impact of that shift assessed. Clearly the process is not quick, easy, or painless. No guarantee exists that including the consumer as a collaborator-in-service will either decrease the demands of society for more and better health care or increase a service-system's capacity to meet those demands. While the mechanisms governing the operation of a health care system merely provide the framework within which people operate, the promise for those who are served and the reward for those who would serve better is that shared responsibility will lead to a more resilient and responsive health care system.

PART IV

PROBLEMS IN PATERNALISM

The voluntary associations described in Part III are ways groups have of getting the things they want. Part IV gives examples of a different way, more characteristic of complex societies, and especially of cities. Paternalism means that a group of people assume certain powers and responsibilities for another group—they feel they know better than others what is good for them and how to bring it about. This broad definition applies to many situations not usually labeled paternalistic; in fact, it applies to many city agencies.

People on the receiving end of paternalistic policy perceive it as such, and often resent it, even when those implementing the policy are not aware of these implications. The recipients cannot express these feelings directly without jeopardizing their hopes of some kind of improvement, so they express them indirectly by urinating in elevators and writing on the walls of new buildings, and breaking the windows of community centers. Those who pay for these buildings are furious at the lack of the gratitude they had anticipated.

In many non-Western societies, mechanisms for redistributing surplus wealth keep class structure from evolving. Despite the graduated income tax and public education, complex societies do have a class structure, and inequalities in wealth and access to knowledge, which bring about the potential for paternalistic relationships. The fact that some people have more than others leads inevitably to conflicts, but the paternalistic approach shortchanges the disadvantaged by co-opting real dissent and freezing the recipients into a crippling status, as was the case with the Papago.

The self-determination that is the opposite of paternalism is a very basic American value. Just like the Grange and the New England Town Meeting, the PTA and the block association are examples of the American "do-it-yourself" philosophy. But this kind of autonomy is incompatible with the centralization that develops in urban life, where there are professions and bureaucracies whose job it is to decide and implement what is best for people. Handing over city administration to professional experts is necessary because of the complexity of urban problems, but it distances people from the decisions that affect their lives.

Most frequently decision-making in urban bureaucracies is so fragmented that the complaint is neglect and inefficiency, but sometimes they are efficient enough to do real damage. Centralization means that decisions are made without people having a voice in them. This process is no less paternalistic because many different types of professionals and agencies, rather than the more personal patron or company manager, make decisions for the community.

The danger of paternalism must not discourage those who are working for social change—it means, however, that they must focus on working with people to find out what they really want and how to bring it about through collaboration.

Part IV offers some examples of the adverse effects of paternalism on people outside the urban United States. Examining this problem in situations where it is more clear-cut will facilitate understanding of similar relationships generated by the class and minority group inequalities and the specialization of complex societies.

Introduction to
Slum Clearance and Family Life in Lagos

In Central Lagos relocation was even more devastating to the residents' livelihoods and social networks than it is in the United States where many people live and work in separate places. In cities in developing countries, where there are few supermarkets or department stores, commerce takes the form of street trading. A street trader depends upon building up a clientele in a central location, and in this case, their community served as that location. The clearance scheme meant the loss not only of their homes, but of their jobs.

The Central Lagos project was strictly a clearance scheme —no new housing was built at public expense on that site. The shabby look of the neighborhood led politicians to consider it a slum. If residents wanted to buy back the bare land where their houses once stood, they had first option but had to pay more than they had been compensated originally. In addition they had the cost of building anew. They were forced into the position of being renters rather than owners for the first time, and of those who moved to the government subsidized rehousing estate, Suru Lere, many were evicted during the first year for not being able to pay rent.

Loss of economic resources disrupted family life because residents could not meet their traditional obligations to those family members who needed help. The visiting of relatives, the main focus of social life in Central Lagos, became much more difficult because family members now lived far apart. Residents of Suru Lere gave up their memberships in family associations, church and social groups because they could no longer afford either the bus fare or the membership subscription. Their lives were impoverished by the loss of family relationships and of those voluntary associations that make city life satisfying.

City officials saw this program as progress because sewers were put in, streets were widened, and housing they regarded as substandard was removed. Makers of public policy are often criticized for not taking into consideration what people want, but in this case the real costs were even more than the people could bear. Ironically, the name Suru Lere means "Patience is rewarded" in Yoruba.

While the results of relocation in cities in the United States are not often as serious as they were for the people of Central Lagos, the loss of social networks connected with a particular neighborhood, as in Boston's West End, is often a consequence unforeseen by urban planners. Judging from the street disturbances and strong resistance to clearance, the residents did anticipate the magnitude of the loss of their economic and social life. Often people do know better than specialists how their own lives will be affected by changes.

---

15. SLUM CLEARANCE AND FAMILY LIFE IN LAGOS

by Peter Marris

Slums are amongst the most obtrusive of social evils. Physical squalor catches the eye; the degradation of human dignity shocks the social reformer, civic pride is outraged, the privileged are uncomfortably reminded of the circumstances in which their fellow countrymen must live. To people who do not live in slums, their demolition seems self-evidently desirable. Yet the slum dwellers themselves often bitterly resent being displaced. Where, as in South Africa, slum clearance is openly undertaken for the protection of the privileged, such

From *Human Organization*, Volume 19, No. 3, Fall 1960, pp. 123–28.

a conflict of interests is not surprising. But the conflict also arises where the welfare of the people to be rehoused is the principal aim of policy.

In Africa, the initiative in slum clearance usually comes from public agencies, which are run by aliens, or the most privileged members of society. They tend to assume that physical squalor must be associated with moral degradation: the slums must be riven with crime, ill-health, a demoralized irresponsibility in family life. But this need not be so. The slum may be merely the longest-settled neighborhood, grown shabby with age, which yet enjoys the most integrated social life of any in the city. The people who live there are not necessarily all impoverished, or humiliated, by their surroundings. Even if they are, they probably cannot afford to live otherwise, and, unless the underlying causes of their poverty are first removed, the attempt to rehouse them at a standard beyond their means will only make them destitute. There is a danger, therefore, that slum clearance schemes will be based on arbitrary assumptions as to how slum-dwellers live, and ought to live; and that they will set standards related more to the social values of the leaders of society, than to the needs and resources of the people to be rehoused. But the more realistically the difficulties are assessed, the more intractable they are likely to appear.

I would like to illustrate the problem by the slum clearance scheme in Lagos, the federal capital of Nigeria, of which I made a study during 1958 and 1959—especially as to its effect on family life. The figures quoted in the first section are based on a sample of the adult population of the area in Central Lagos scheduled for demolition as slums; and in the second, on two samples of heads of households, in four streets of the slum area and in the rehousing estate, respectively.

THE PEOPLE OF CENTRAL LAGOS

The part of Central Lagos to be cleared as slums has been settled for two or more generations. The streets are shown in their present form on a map of 1885. The houses would have been built originally by families for their own use, although many have later been divided, or let to tenants. A few still standing follow the design of a traditional Yoruba compound, the rooms surrounding an open courtyard on four sides. But, in more recent building, the courtyard has dwindled to a passage leading from the street to a yard, often with rooms opening onto it from one or two sides, and lavatories and washplaces at the back. In these yards, or on a verandah overlooking the street, the women do most of their housework. The rooms are sometimes so full of bed and baggage that there is hardly space to put a chair. In four streets of Central Lagos which I investigated, there were 1.9 adults and 1.6 children to each room—3.5 people in all. But such cramped quarters are manageable because the occupants do little but sleep and make love there.

The houses are shabby—the walls patched, the roofs leaky, the ceilings blackened with smoke. But some have solid walls, well-made doors and windows, and a concrete floor raised above the ground. They have suffered as much from neglect as from dilapidation.

According to Yoruba custom,[1] the children of the founder of a family property occupy it, together with their wives and children, and their descendants after them. The daughters have much the same rights as the sons, except that they would be expected to live with their husband in his family house. In fact, there seem to be only a few family properties still occupied in this way in Lagos. Usually some rooms are let, some are occupied by the descendants of the founder, and others by more distant relatives, for whom those with rights in the house are responsible. For example, in the four streets I studied in detail, out of twenty-nine properties, eleven were occupied only by tenants, fourteen by both owners and tenants, and four entirely by the family which owned it. About 60 per cent of the present residents are tenants.

The tenants in Central Lagos, however, are long settled there. More than half of those interviewed had lived in Lagos

[1] The Yoruba account for 70 per cent of the population of Lagos, and were the original settlers. Customary land-holding in Lagos is therefore according to traditional Yoruba practice. The Yoruba, a people of five millions, are the dominant tribal group of the Lagos hinterland.

for over twenty years, and nearly half had occupied the same rooms for more than ten years. Nine-tenths of the owners and their relatives were born in Lagos, half of them in the house in which they still lived. Even amongst the tenants who had taken their rooms most recently, the majority had occupied them for at least six years. The population is the most stable in Lagos.

The slum clearance area is at the heart of Lagos commercial life. It lies between the two main shopping streets; surrounded by the largest markets in cloth, vegetables, meat, and poultry, enamel and earthenware, herbs, fancy goods and fruit; and within a few minutes of the great importing houses. Much of the working population of Lagos passes every day by its narrow lanes. The people of the neighbourhood earn their living by the commerce of the city. The men are traders, importers and exporters, shopkeepers, dockers, and market porters; drivers, watchmen, clerks, or mechanics for the foreign firms; or craftsmen who often deal in goods on the side— bicycle repairers selling secondhand machines and tyres, spray painters selling paint, blacksmiths buying up used tins and making them into cheap oil lamps. The women nearly all trade.

Traders and many of the craftsmen work on their own account, and depend for their livelihood on attracting a group of regular customers to whom they are readily available. Some of the labourers, too, are only casually employed, and must be in easy reach of employers who may be hiring men for the day. So, more than half the working population are likely to earn less, at least for a while, if they are moved from the neighbourhood where they have established themselves.

Two-thirds of the men earn between £6 and £20 a month, the labourers earning least. Traders and craftsmen have the highest proportion of both the poorest and most prosperous. The women traders, however, usually make substantially less than the men: the majority have a profit of less than £10 a month, although there were still 13 per cent amongst those I interviewed with incomes over £20.

The people of Central Lagos are, therefore, largely dependent upon their location at the centre of commerce for their livelihood. And because they have, on the whole, been long settled there, an integrated pattern of social and family life has grown up. The affection and sense of mutual obligation of the family group is the outstanding loyalty of Lagos social life.

Nigerians are brought up to regard the needs of their kinfolk as their first responsibility; they support their mothers and fathers in their old age, and often elderly aunts or cousins as well. They contribute to the marriage payment of a younger brother, bring up their nephews and nieces, help out their married sisters. More than half the people interviewed in Central Lagos were spending at least a tenth of their income on help to their relatives. Without this family loyalty, there would be no one to care for the old, the sick, the widows and orphans, no one to set men on their feet when they were out of work, or to pass on to younger brothers and sisters the advantages of an education for which, as likely as not, the family has paid. For, as yet, public social services in Nigeria are few. The family group collects its dues, and distributes its funds to those in need; it gives its members at least an ultimate security against the misfortunes of life.

Besides these personal obligations, the family displays its unity in frequent celebrations—naming ceremonies for a newborn child, marriages, funerals, anniversaries, a sendoff for a brother going overseas—and to these each branch of the family will contribute its share. A group of relatives will often choose a costume for the occasion, and symbolise their unity by appearing in this uniform—a pretty but expensive custom. There are also regular meetings—sometimes weekly, or on a Sunday of each month—when the difficulties of members are discussed, disputes settled, and the progress of the family reviewed. Many meetings raise a small subscription, minutes are taken, and officers elected from time to time; they are, therefore, formal gatherings, comprising from half-a-dozen to fifty people or more. In some families, the subscription will be put aside toward the building or repair of the family house, or even the running of a corporate business in the name of the founder. Two-thirds of the men and women interviewed in Central Lagos belonged to families which held such meetings regularly in the course of a year.

But the day-to-day visits exchanged by relatives strengthen

the unity of the family group more than do these formal meetings. News is passed on, problems discussed as they arise, and the old people are able to live comfortably on the small presents of cash or kind brought for them by the kinsfolk who call during the day. Although it is less common now for all a man's descendants to be together in one house, the families of Central Lagos live, for the most part, no more than ten or fifteen minutes walk from each other. Tenants tend to have fewer kin near them than owners, but the longer they have lived in Lagos, the more likely that they will have attracted other members of their family to the town. Amongst those interviewed in Central Lagos, 32 per cent of all those whose mother was still living shared the same house with her, 38 per cent had at least one of their brothers or sisters in the same house, 23 per cent one of their half brothers or sisters. About two-thirds had one or more of their brothers or sisters, and of their parents, living on Lagos Island within a mile of them.

Most of the people in this part of Lagos, therefore, have many relatives nearby. They may also be members of mutual benefit societies, Bible study classes, Moslem organisations, or associations of people from their town or village of origin—all of which flourish. Everyone who belongs to such a group has a status, rights and obligations, and enjoys the sense of security which comes from these.

All Nigerians, I think, are very loyal to their family group —they regard their membership in it with pride and affection, and derive a deep sense of emotional security from it. I believe that some of the emotional security which a European would look for in marriage, a Nigerian expects to find rather in a more generalised relationship with his kin.

Because of this emotional and economic dependence upon the kin group, there is less emphasis on loyalty between husbands and wives. Marriage is more of a contract, with limited obligations. Husband and wife, recognising the attachment of the other to his own relatives, tend to trust each other less, and share less in common. Feelings are not deeply committed. The marriage may break down when money problems or the claims of other loyalties press upon it, especially in a polygamous household. When a man has to share his income amongst several wives, the place of any one of them is less secure. Jealousies and rivalries may lead to irreconcilable quarrels. A woman may prefer to return to her own people, rather than suffer the introduction of a new wife into the household —particularly if her husband did not consult her beforehand. Nearly a fifth of those interviewed in Central Lagos had contracted a marriage which failed, some several times. These risks make a woman protect herself by a wariness in marriage, and she tends to look on it as a contract which must be exploited before it is dishonoured.

Even when there has been no quarrel, married couples do not always live together; a woman past child-bearing sometimes prefers to return to her own family. A third of the wives interviewed in Central Lagos did not live with their husbands, a fifth of the husbands with none of their wives. Because of this, children may grow up apart from one of their parents, and sometimes from both; young children are sent for training to a brother, a sister, or a grandmother, where they will be expected to be useful about the house, and less spoilt. A quarter of the sample had some of their children under sixteen living elsewhere. Since the children spend more of their time outside their parents' household, they get used to regarding themselves as members of a family group. To protect themselves against the rivalries of a polygamous household, and the instability of the relationship between their parents, the children of the same mother tend to be drawn together with an enduring affection. As children grow up, therefore, it is natural for them to place their strongest affections and loyalties in the family group, rather than in a relationship with one man or woman. Thus, although most marriages are successful, there is less feeling of dependence in them. There is also less financial dependence.

A woman cannot allow her own and her children's welfare to rest only on what her husband can provide. Wages are low, employment insecure, traders are at the mercy of fluctuations in the market; illness, for lack of medical care, may be serious and protracted. There is no guarantee that her husband will always be able to support her. He may—with her consent or not—take other wives, and his resources will have to go all the further. So every woman tries to secure an independent income from a shop, or dressmaking, or, most commonly, from trade. Unless her parents have provided for her, she will expect a sum of money from her husband to buy a stock in trade, from which she may make anything from a few shillings to fifty pounds or more a month. Her profit is her own, an independent income which protects her against losing her husband, and enables her to fulfill her obligations to her own family. Her husband is saved responsibility for her personal expenses, and she may be able to help him out of her earnings if he finds himself in difficulties. The trading of women is, therefore, an essential part of the household economy and, but for it, she would be an unequal and vulnerable partner in marriage, and would have nothing to contribute to her own kin. A woman may be at her market stall from early morning until dusk, and this, rather than her home, gets her best attention.

THE CONSEQUENCES OF SLUM CLEARANCE

The slum clearance scheme requires the wholesale demolition of the neighbourhoods of Central Lagos whose way of life has been described. Families are offered tenancies in a rehousing estate, at Suru Lere in the suburbs, in terraced cottages of one to four rooms. The owners of the property are compensated and have the opportunity to repurchase plots in Central Lagos as they are developed, but the price considerably exceeds the amount of compensation. At present, it seems unlikely that any of the owners formerly resident in Central Lagos will be able to afford to return there. The population of Central Lagos will probably be permanently dispersed by the scheme. Their rehabilitation presents serious difficulties, both for their family life and their livelihood.

The rehousing estate provides well-built and well-spaced houses, with gardens, quiet, running water, and proper sanitation. But it is five miles from the centre of Lagos, at the end of an uncomfortable sixpenny bus ride. So those who moved to the estate were much further from their relatives in Central Lagos. Also many of those whose houses have been pulled down have not gone to the estate at all, preferring to rent cheaper accommodation on the outskirts of the town;

or they have gone to stay with relatives, or have evicted tenants from other property which they own. A young clerk, who had been moved from a large family house, told me:

> When we were about to come here, most of our people didn't want to come to this bush—they call this place bush —they think there are bad spirits here. So the proportion of us who came here, in short, was only two of us out of twenty. The rest went to rent places in E. B. or Idi Oro [suburbs of Lagos]. They think these houses here are not the kind of houses in which we Africans live—you know we live in groups, not one here, one there. So I have only one relative here. She is a woman selling cloth, and since she came here, the trade has flopped. This woman is too fat, she can't be going to Lagos every time on the bus, so she had to give up. She is even thinking of quitting because of the rent. They have a family house in E. B., and they have just quitted the tenant, who has been there a long time. Now she has to leave this place and go to live there. She has a brother too; that one did not come here. He could not afford the rentage in E. B., not to think of Lagos, and has to go to Agege [a town fifteen miles distant]. He is a pensioner, and if you see his condition now you will pity him.

A comparison of the two samples of households interviewed shows how much the family group had been disrupted. The proportion of householders at Suru Lere with their mother, a brother or sister living within a mile of them dropped by more than half.

Because they live at a greater distance, the residents on the rehousing estate also see their relatives less often. They pay fewer visits: leaving early and returning late, they make as many calls as they can on their way to and from work. Once home, they are usually too tired to go out again, even if they could afford it. And they receive fewer visitors. Many I interviewed explained that their relatives found Suru Lere too isolated: fares were too expensive, they lacked time for the journey, tired of waiting for the bus, or were even unable to find the address when they arrived.

> In Lagos you'd have your supper, and you'd think, I'd like to go and see my sister. And you'd come back in an

hour's time and tell your wife, I've been to see my sister, see my aunt, see my brother . . . now sometimes for a month I don't see them.

When I was in Lagos they were with me. We live in the same street. Old wife's family, new wife's family, we see each other every day. In Lagos you see everybody nearly every day. Do you see any of my family visiting me here?

On Saturday I made 5 shillings gain, and I ran to see my mother. I've not seen her since Saturday and God knows when I shall see her again. She wept when I was to leave, because she didn't want to leave me, and she is afraid to come here. When I was in Lagos there was not a day I don't see her—if I couldn't go in the morning I go at night.

So the residents at Suru Lere could no longer maintain so easily the day-to-day contact with their families, and the proportion who saw them less often than once a month also rose sharply.

The more formal cohesion of the family also suffered. Sixty-one per cent of those interviewed in Central Lagos were members of a regular family meeting, but only 27 per cent at Suru Lere—either because they no longer attended, or because the meetings had been abandoned with the demolition of the family property. Even where the meeting was still held, fewer came. One man remarked:

All these meetings I told you of were when we were in Lagos; when the slum came, it scattered us. [He was the most senior of his family, and the meeting was still held, at his home on the Estate. But it was now fortnightly instead of weekly, and attendance had dropped from thirty to five.] When we came here, you only get those of the same father. Last Saturday we had a meeting, there were only five. But before there would be my aunt, her children, my brother's children . . . This place is far, number one. Money to come, number two.

Slum clearance, therefore, means that family groups tend to be disrupted. This can be especially hard for old people who had lived in family property and been cared for by relatives around them. Their relatives elsewhere are no longer so aware of their needs, and they themselves cannot afford the fare to go and ask them for help. The system of mutual support begins to break down. Many of the people on the estate, who were used to giving regular help to their relatives, could no longer afford it. Although rents on the estate are subsidised, they are still, on the whole, more than was being paid before, partly because in Central Lagos, where tenancies are of long standing, rents are exceptionally low; and partly because households occupy more space on the estate than they had before. The former owners are usually paying rent for the first time in their lives. In Central Lagos the average rent of the accommodation occupied by the tenants interviewed was £2. 1s. 6d., on the rehousing estate £2. 7s. 9d. But the cost of transport worried them even more than the rent. It was the most universal complaint—fares to work, to get their children to school, their wives to market. It also raised their expenses indirectly: the men had to buy a midday meal at work, since they could not afford to come home, and prices in the local shops were higher because of transport charges. Apart from the shops, where prices were high, there was no market. Fifty-seven per cent of those interviewed were spending upwards of £1 a month on fares—a tenth of the income of over half the sample. Some of the men who worked late into the night, and had to depend on taxis, spent over £5 a month on fares.

To make ends meet, they could no longer be so generous in helping their kin. In Central Lagos, 35 per cent of the household heads made regular monthly allotments of at least £2 to relatives apart from their immediate family, but at Suru Lere only 13 per cent could do as much. Because they could no longer contribute, they were sometimes shy of visiting relatives whom they had been used to helping. One woman, for instance, told me she had an especially affectionate relationship with a young half-sister, who was still at school.

> She treats me like a father, she asks me for anything she wants—school books, money, clothes. I don't go to see her now—she's sure to ask me for something, and I can't afford it. Once in a month or two months perhaps I go, when I can scrape together five or ten shillings.

Their families apart, they also tended to give up entertainment and their membership of benefit societies, church groups, and social clubs, because they could no longer afford either the fare or the subscription. One young man, a salesman who was earning a better income than most, remarked:

> I was a member of four clubs when I was in Lagos. I used to attend the functions regularly, almost every night. I've never been again since I came here. Even table tennis—I don't think I could hold a bat now. And cinema—I used to go to the cinema every night with my wife. But even if we could get transport, I don't think we have enough allowance for the pictures again. We used to attend dances in Lagos too, but we don't do it now. And I went to church every Sunday in Lagos too, every day in the Lenten season. Since we've been here, I don't think I've been to church more than twice.

The higher cost of living in the rehousing estate is much more difficult to meet, because so many of the households earn less as well. Traders and independent craftsmen lose most of their business when they move. Few if any of their former customers are willing to lose time and money on a long bus ride, when they can take their orders more conveniently elsewhere. The population of the estate itself is too small and too dispersed to support many traders or craftsmen, especially as most people go into Central Lagos every day and continue to buy there, where the choice is wider and prices lower. The estate lies off the main roads and attracts few outsiders. Moreover, the people already established in the neighbourhood have pre-empted the best sites for market stalls along the road to the city centre. Even those on the estate who still work from a shop or stall in Central Lagos find that business suffers. They are no longer accessible to customers at home; lose time in travelling and cannot supervise their apprentices so thoroughly; and since they cannot carry their stock home every night, have now expenses in storage or guards.

Most of the people interviewed on the estate who had been traders or independent craftsmen were therefore in real difficulties, some destitute. A shoemaker I went to interview greeted me with the comment,

> I am alone working. Alone "playing" I should say. When I was in Lagos I would reluctantly give you half an hour.

Now, if you want five hours . . . Before I moved here, I
was first class shoemaker having shoe-making machine. I
had a shop—that was Broad Street—and if you see the condition of my shop in Lagos you will like to repair your
shoes there. It was my father's occupation so I have sufficient tools. When I was there, I had a certain contract with
the Police force, and another from the Elder Dempster
Company for the crews' shoes. And the crews themselves
when they came from England, they bring their shoe for
repair. Broad Street is not far from the Customs. Murray
Street [where he lived] is even nearer, only one street cross
us. All now—nothing from there now. [He used to make
£200 or £300 a year.] Since I came here, not sufficient
money to rent a shop here, let alone work there. This is
what I have since Monday—it is 4s.6d., and when I took it
to the owner he said, "Didn't you know? This is not like
Lagos, I will come for it when I have got to have money."
From Monday now, I've got one threepence, this morning.
If you look at the street now, you will not see a single man.
They have all gone to Lagos, and take their shoes there for
repair . . . This is not a place, but a punishment from
God.

A butcher who had made 20s. to 30s. a day in Lagos, selling from a market stall, had used up all his capital on fares
and meeting the higher cost of living, and his trade declined
until he was virtually destitute.

Everything has changed against me. I've never had anything like this happen to me since I was born. It seems
like being taken from happiness to misery.

A dressmaker had been almost as unfortunate:

I printed cards out and gave them, but they say they
can't come the long journey, there are so many tailors in
Lagos. All these people here, they go to Lagos to buy, give
all their business to traders in Lagos. They only come here
to sleep. There's nothing at all here. They say we should
take one of the shops here—but there's no one to patronise.
I cut out paper patterns for the girls here sometimes, and
that's all, except baby dresses occasionally—two or three
shillings. Business is paralyzed.

Some of the skilled workers had given up working on their
own account since they moved to the estate; and many of

the traders and craftsmen probably avoided the estate in the first place. Nearly half the men interviewed in Central Lagos were self-employed, but only a quarter at Suru Lere—and most of these were earning less. As a whole, the income of self-employed men had fallen by an average of £8 a month since their move to the estate. Since it is more difficult for a woman to find a paid job, they suffered even more; the income of the women interviewed fell by an average of £10.

The wives of the men interviewed were equally affected. A quarter had given up any attempt to trade, while as many had lost most of their business but still struggled, rather hopelessly, to scrape together a few shillings in the month. There were four times as many wives earning nothing on the estate, as in the households interviewed in Central Lagos. They had to depend more on their husbands, and the men at Suru Lere did, in fact, give more substantial allowances to their wives— mostly at the expense of other family obligations.

The rehousing estate had, therefore, all the disadvantages to a trader that its isolation and dispersed population would suggest. Central Lagos is the hub of the city, alive from early morning until late at night: "It is Canaan to us," said a woman trader, "a land of milk and honey." Suru Lere is deserted for most of the day, and its only thoroughfare skirts rather than crosses the estate. So there were fewer traders at Suru Lere, and more women not working at all, and those who still traded much made less by it. In Central Lagos, the average profit of all the traders in the households interviewed was £11. 12s. 4d.: on the rehousing estate it was £4. 1s. 9d. As one old lady was driven to exclaim: "May God deliver me out of this place."

As a whole, therefore, the tenants on the estate earned less and paid out more than before they were moved. The amenities of the estate, its gardens and peace, sanitation and piped water, were luxuries they could not appreciate. Many of the families had got into debt since they arrived, especially in arrears of rent, and were haunted by the fear of eviction. Harassed by financial worries, some households disintegrated.

Life on the estate, with fewer wives at work, husbands paying them more generous allowances, and interfering relatives at a distance, ought to have encouraged marriage: and there were several young couples who enjoyed their new independence and privacy. But more often, far from husband and wife drawing closer together, they were forced to separate. Unable to meet the expenses of suburban life, some of the husbands sent their wives home to their families and distributed their children amongst relatives who could care for them. Wives, finding no opportunity for trade, left to live with their own relatives nearer the centre of the city; others simply deserted when their husbands could no longer support them. One man, who had been particularly unlucky, said of his junior wife, "I hadn't a penny to put down for her, so she had to desert me, she said she couldn't stay here to starve." Another man had sent his wife to her mother on Lagos Island. "I can't keep her here when I can't maintain her." He went to see her once a month. "It's no use going when you can only put your hand in an empty pocket." A van driver said:

> When I was in Lagos, I never pay for house, I had money. I could have financed my wife with something to sell. Now the house is pulled down it change everything. She is every time crying, fighting, worrying me for money. Even yesterday I told her to quit if she kept on worrying me for money. I can't steal.

Of the married men 27 per cent had been divorced at some time, an appreciably higher proportion than in the Central Lagos sample, and at least in some cases the quarrel had arisen out of the difficulties they experienced since they were moved.

Even when there had been no quarrel, husbands and wives spent more time apart. In Central Lagos 81 per cent of the married people saw their husband or wife daily; at Suru Lere only 64 per cent. More of the young children, too, were living outside the household. The more scattered the family group, the more difficult it is to fulfill obligations without absence from home. And the poorer people are, the greater the strain on the loyalty of husband or wife, and the competing claims of marriage and kin are less easily reconciled.

It would be wrong to imply, however, that all the families in the estate were either miserable, or in danger of disintegration. A third of those I interviewed preferred it on the whole to where they had lived before. They liked the houses, the quiet in which to study, it gave some of the young couples the chance of a private life out of reach of interfering neighbours and relatives. But those who were best pleased with their new surroundings were least characteristic of the people of Central Lagos for whom the estate was planned: they tended to be immigrants from distant parts of Nigeria, and in the more senior clerical posts. For the rest, the people of the estate felt they had acquired the amenities of a modern house at a sacrifice of their family life and livelihood, a change which had been forced upon them and one which they would not have made from choice.

CONCLUSION

Slum clearance raises the fundamental problem: how can you destroy a neighbourhood physically, without destroying at the same time the livelihood and way of life of the people who have settled there? If these are destroyed, the clearance of slums is likely to do more harm than good.

If compulsory rehousing is to be just, and a benefit to those rehoused, it must, I believe, fulfill two conditions:

(1) The people must be able to afford it. In Africa, this must mean that it will cost them no more to live in their new houses than their old, since very few people have money enough to pay for better housing. Those who can afford it and want to spend their money in this way will have already provided for themselves. If people are forced to pay for housing they cannot afford, their poverty will oblige them to restrict their participation in social life. Above all, it will withdraw them from their family, and this, in Africa especially, can cause great unhappiness.

(2) They must be able to re-establish their pattern of life in the new surroundings. They must not be too far distant from their kin, nor their work, and the same range of economic activities must be open to them. And their new homes must be so designed that they can be adapted to their way of life. That is to say, if they have depended for their livelihood on being at the centre of trade, they must be rehoused where they have the same chances of custom, or where there are alternative ways of earning a living open to them.

These two conditions are likely to be very difficult to fulfill in practice. The second condition can most easily be realised by rehousing the people on the site which has been cleared, but if they are to be less crowded than before, the buildings will have to be of several storeys. In Lagos, at least, this would have been very expensive indeed and the cost could not have been recovered in rents. To provide for the people in the suburbs, as in Lagos, brings down the cost of housing only to increase the cost of fares, and makes it very much more difficult to prevent the disruption of family groups and economic relationships. New markets must be developed, new opportunities of employment provided; and the new estate must be able to absorb not only those removed from the slums, but relatives who wish to settle with them or near them.

Lastly, however the problem is tackled, it is likely to cost a lot of public money. The tendency is therefore to make the people who are rehoused pay for some of the cost themselves, on the grounds that they are, after all, enjoying a higher standard of housing, and the scheme is for their benefit. I believe this to be unjust: if they have to pay for it, it will not be to their benefit, for the reasons I have given. If their interests only are to be considered, it would be better not to rehouse them at all. If slums are to be cleared for reasons of national prestige, the cost is a fair charge on the public purse.[2]

But if slum clearance is costly, difficult to achieve without hardship and cannot fairly be charged to the people rehoused, then is it perhaps better to concentrate first on other equally urgent problems? Where the population of a town is growing so fast, overcrowding may well be more effectively stopped by building up new neighbourhoods as yet undeveloped, than by displacing those already settled. The worst housing can meanwhile be gradually improved and rebuilt as opportunity arises. After all, it will be some while before the people of Africa can afford what to us seems a minimum standard of housing. Meanwhile, I think they value more the social amenities of their lives.

---

[2] In a recent debate in the Federal Parliament, reasons of national prestige were in fact given by the minister responsible for Lagos affairs as the first justification of slum clearance.

Introduction to
Resurgent Patronage and Lagging Bureaucracy in a Papago Off-Reservation Community

Employees of big companies in Cali were quickly able to take advantage of patronage and union benefits and conform to the expectations their employers had for their advancement in an impersonal bureaucracy. No ethnic groups were given special consideration in Cali factories. In contrast, the Papago used their special relationship over the years to avoid conforming to sudden company expectations of sobriety, punctuality, and following rules. The copper company saw many acts like refusing promotions and refusing to participate in union activities as inexplicable. But in fact these acts are part of a pattern which perpetuates their special status, even though it means accepting a poor image in the eyes of the company. Ethnic groups in cities may adopt this strategy, whether consciously or unconsciously, to take advantage of a special status once it has been proffered.

Indian identity became associated in the eyes of the company with being a "bad worker." Because the copper company tolerated absenteeism for thirty-five years, the Papago have learned to consider getting away with it their right. The reason they are able to sustain this indulgent relationship is because the copper company feels obligated to maintain a quota of 10 per cent Papago employees. This sense of guilt and obligation is clearly useful to the Indians, and the source of cheap labor is useful to the company.

Once the employer has entered into a paternalistic relationship, he has trouble getting out of it because the group receiving the privilege wants to perpetuate it. The copper company thought that the Indians would eventually learn the values of the impersonal bureaucracy, but turnover rate among

Indian employees is still very high, and very little promotion has occurred even though there is a double standard regarding literacy, and leniency in judging test performances. The Indians are still fulfilling ingrained expectations the company had laid out for them decades ago, and a sudden reversal of policy had very little impact.

The copper company was mistaken to think that paternalism could provide the beginnings of advancement within the system, because the transition from a special status to impersonal standards is difficult if the group feels it has to give up benefits. Furthermore, the Indians were never told that new expectations would eventually be enforced. An urban bureaucracy that exempts some of its clientele from certain requirements, even in an effort to overcome years of inequitable treatment, runs the risk of not being able to change back to uniform standards. It may also be doing a disservice to the group so favored; the prolonged indulgence of drunkenness and absenteeism did not help the Papago improve their economic status by gaining new skills.

---

16. RESURGENT PATRONAGE AND LAGGING BUREAUCRACY IN A PAPAGO OFF-RESERVATION COMMUNITY

by Jack O. Waddell

American Indians have long been used to adapting their behavior to patronistic institutions, but it is increasingly expected that they should transfer habit patterns to bureaucratic institutions. This essay examines a particular case in which Papago Indians, accustomed to a patron/client pattern, are

From *Human Organization*, Volume 29, No. 1, Spring 1970, pp. 37–42.

being asked to acquire behavior patterns more appropriate to a bureaucratic institution.

Foster has defined patron/client dyadic contracts as relationships between individuals of different socioeconomic status who relate to each other in a vertical order of power and whose relationships and obligations are asymmetrical. This is the archetypical form of institutionalized patron relationship. Wolf refers to another type of relationship that is likewise vertical and asymmetrical but where the relationships are polyadic and single-stranded, or directed toward one major task. This is a typically bureaucratic type of institutionalized social relationship. As Wolf notes, however, the single-stranded interest is frequently transformed into a series of many-stranded coalitions which emphasize benevolence and goodwill at the interpersonal level, thus preserving patronistic bonds. The social function of such coalitions is to maximize the single-stranded institutional objectives by reducing the organization's impersonal dimension. Where an organization is built upon an ideology of vertical, condescending patronage, the various interests are held together by the patronistic considerations which have been built into the formal structure.

On the other hand, in large complex institutional structures, where formal, single-stranded coalitions based upon vertical polyadic relations are more likely to occur as a function of the bigness and complexity of the organization, "benevolent" condescending coalitions between unequals are likely to be limited because they are not directly functional to the goals of the institution.

Particularly in state systems, however, the bigness and complexity of bureaucratic organizations, both public and private, tend to be evaluated as at least temporarily inappropriate for resolving the malintegration and inequalities that exist between the society's segments. Spicer has sought to pinpoint micro-processes of directed change involving coalitions or structural linkages between the bureaucratic planning segments and recipient societal segments. While Spicer uses the United States Government's involvements with the conquered aborigines of the United States as his central case, he is interested in developing a basis for comparing or evaluating developmental change in which a dominant segment of a state system seeks to reduce structural inconsistencies between certain parts of the society and, by means of structural intervention, correct the malintegration of the segments and thereby improve the efficiency of the whole system. As Civil Rights legislation, Urban Renewal programs, Head Start, and other public and private programs directed toward various social class or ethnic segments reveal, structural linkages as planned and initially implemented seem never to be able to operate on a completely bureaucratic basis; benevolent concern for the object-segment is usually manifest in the structural linkage created. This is largely due to an awareness of the disproportionate access to social and economic power that the planned-for segments have traditionally encountered. It is not surprising that in spite of cries of "tokenism" and other overt expressions of resentment these segments persist in their patterns of dependence on the condescending patronage built into the bureaucratic programs. The widespread malintegration of segments in a complex industrial state system committed to an "equal opportunity" ethic, in addition to having well-established cultural traditions based on what Cohen calls "slave-master" values, is without question a common phenomenon in the modern world, one that needs to be specifically described in a number of local settings.

The unique history of a particular bureaucratic organization, with "survivals" of patronage relationships that are giving way to the ideology characteristic of the single-stranded, or "pure" bureaucratic type, is presented here.

COPPER CORPORATION AND COPPER TOWN

The case in question is located in Copper Town, a small mining community in southwestern Arizona, where Copper Corporation operates a sizable open pit copper mine. The American Indians involved are predominantly Papagos. The town, with a population of 7,000, is a "company town" whose very existence is dependent upon the operations of Copper Corporation. Directly east of Copper Town are the almost three million acres of the main Papago reservation.

The population of Copper Town is about 65 per cent Anglo-Americans, 25 per cent Mexican-Americans, and 10 per cent Indian-Americans. Each of these ethnic groups has its own smaller community, or subcommunity. Like the other communities, the Indian community is not a single homogeneous entity either residentially or occupationally.

The present mining operations in the Copper Town area date back to the middle of the nineteenth century. Although the company does not have accurate records prior to 1936, there is some evidence that Papagos have always been available to perform the "muscle" and menial jobs that were particularly important in the premechanization period of the mining operation. They were geographically convenient and were willing to work on a daily basis, primarily in the pit operations. Since 1936, however, the number and percentage of Indians on the company's payroll have declined fairly steadily.

Company records indicate that as late as 1940, only 7 per cent of the total Indian work force was listed as skilled. It is therefore likely that prior to 1936 almost the entire Indian labor force was unskilled. Since 1940, the number of semiskilled Indian workers and machine operators has increased considerably, but there has been little change at the more highly skilled levels.

Before the Depression, the majority of the Papagos on the payroll lived temporarily in the mining area while working, but there was no organized attention on the part of the company to the organization or welfare of the Indian families. Long before the mining operations began, Papagos had a tradition of camping in temporary makeshift dwellings at convenient sites within their territory; and the first Papago mine employees merely continued this temporary and intermittent pattern of encampment while away from their home rancherias.

Indians thus were a plentiful source of unskilled labor. They did not have a very high standard of living, but they were sufficiently introduced to the money economy to make the mining operation at least temporarily attractive. The Papagos did not have to be concerned with keeping steady year-round jobs; they could come and go as they pleased. If they needed a little cash, they could go to work on the track gangs; but they need not worry if, after a few days of work, they decided to get drunk, or go back to the reservation, or simply to quit work, since there was no great anxiety about putting in regular hours either to keep a job or to meet an as yet nonexistent "middle-class" level of material needs, or to render sober and dedicated service to a single employer. They had few skills to market, but the mining operation did make use of their adaptability to the arid Southwestern climate. Where Anglos might find both the work and the climate unattractive and be prompted to move on, the Indians had roots in the area and could be counted on. If some Indian workers failed to turn out or quit their jobs, there were always others ready to pick up a few days of work.

All of the first Indians to work for Copper Corporation were in the same occupational status: unskilled laborers hired to lay tracks or remove the tons of rock formations, waste, and ores. There were therefore very few even relatively permanent families in the Indian Village. The company had little incentive to invest in the extra-work interests of its Indian laborers when the largest proportion of them were highly transient; there was no need for any highly institutionalized relationships.

Individual Papagos, however, began to enter into patron-like dyads with the permanent Anglo residents of Copper Town who were primarily responsible for founding and organizing the mining interests. These Anglos befriended certain families in Indian Village, showing an interest in their welfare and building up informal obligatory relationships which operated to insure perpetual family connections with the mining operation. It is inconceivable that so many clear-cut networks of linkages with specific Papago villages could have developed over the pre-Depression years without these patronistic dyads. The single-stranded interest of exploiting Indian labor to extract ores was the primary objective from the beginning; but the persistence of this source of common labor could not have been insured without these many-stranded coalitions, or patronage dyads between certain Anglos and certain Papago families.

The mine closed down during the Depression. When it later resumed operations, the company sent trucks to reservation villages to round up former employees who wanted to return to work at the mine. By 1936, there was a sizable, relatively permanent and "steady" community of Indians involved in the mining operations. And the New Deal concerns of the Franklin Roosevelt years were becoming evident in Copper Corporation as elsewhere in the United States. The growing mechanization of industry, the rising social, economic, and educational privileges for America's "poor," and many other factors were instrumental in compelling Copper Corporation to formalize its relationships with Indian workers and to take new kinds of interests in this group upon which it had depended for many years.

In 1936, the company began to pay formal attention to the welfare of the Indian community and to plan and build houses for Indian employees and their families. As the planned village has grown, the trend has been toward different kinds and qualities of houses, depending upon the person's status in the company. In fact, the company sees the community as one way to encourage incentive and to provide motivation for the more traditional Papagos to adopt the standards of living and behavior of the few Papagos who have attained higher status in the company and who are rewarded by being offered the opportunity to rent bigger and nicer homes.

Company-directed interests in many areas of the community's social and economic life similarly express the paternalism of Copper Corporation toward its employees. These include the company hospital clinic, the cooperative store, company interests in the educational standards of its employees and their children, community organization and leadership, and a concern with the regulation of behavioral standards in such areas as marriage requirements, socioeconomic upgrading, the inculcation of necessary motivational values, and the elimination of undesirable or detrimental behavior. These facilities and services are extended to members of the community at large, but numerous examples clearly indicate that they are particularly geared to Indians.

In these post-Depression activities Copper Corporation, in effect, institutionalized the existing many-stranded patronistic and dyadic coalitions to strengthen its own single-stranded interest. The company thus became the major patron, taking an interest in its employees in much the same way that single individuals had done earlier. Eventually the company began to recognize that this paternalistic outlook was inconsistent with company ideals and expectations based on the rational bureaucratic model, and organizational efforts were made to deal with what were becoming serious incompatibilities.

One incompatibility, for example, is occasioned by the use of a formal battery of literacy and aptitude tests, to motivate employees to elevate their expectations and upgrade themselves, as well as to insure equal and impartial handling of all applicants for limited statuses. Most of the Indians are unprepared to pass such qualifying tests. Applicants from all other ethnic groups are eliminated from consideration if they fail the literacy tests. But in order to permit Indians to compete for available jobs instead of being eliminated completely, they are given a number of special considerations, including the chance to take the test over several times and greater leniency in interpreting their test results. Or if an Indian does pass, he is hired right away while members of other ethnic groups may have to wait in line. In this way, particular structural linkages with Indian interests are maintained by the company in order not to eliminate them from the system entirely.

Absenteeism is treated in much the same manner. Special considerations for Papago attendance patterns have been institutionalized and are part of the condescending interim structure developed to handle the situation *until* the patterns are eventually corrected and the operation can continue in terms of its bureaucratic ideal. Actually, the company has rather rigid and well-defined rules for dealing with the kind of absenteeism that is a prevailing characteristic of Indian employees. Warning slips are issued for third, fourth, and fifth absences in a year's time, with penalties or firing after the fifth warning. However, since the company is formally committed to an ethnic balance which includes a 10 per cent Indian representation in the work force, it must make some special concessions since the Indian 10 per cent amounts to about 25 per cent of the mine's turnover. Thus, Indians who have not exceeded their fourth absence or second warning slip after a year's work, have that year's absences removed from their record so they can start the next year with a clean slate. Indians are increasingly "learning the system" well enough to make sure they do not exceed their quota of absences. The company employment agent also admits that the rules are bent a bit if certain Indians with good work records exceed the absentee limit.

The company has recently been sincerely concerned about treating the Indians equally, but it cannot neglect the fact that Indians are still dealt with as if they needed special condescending attention to help them fit their traditional patterns into the goals and expectations of the company. A further dilemma arises because the Indians interpret bureaucratic attempts to institutionalize equality and fair treatment of all employees as efforts on the part of Copper Corporation to discriminate against Indians. The company is now just a step away from a completely bureaucratic commitment with respect to hiring procedures which insure that only the best qualified will be placed, regardless of ethnic background. Those who make it, including a few Indians, will do so on the basis of standardized performance on tests or on jobs as they advance up the scale of occupational statuses. As this occurs, the company will have serious problems in maintaining its 65 per cent Anglo, 25 per cent Mexican-American, 10 per cent Indian employment ratio. There are already indications that the Indian representation is dropping and that the Indians who remain are qualifying for ascent of the bureaucratic occupational status scale by means of formal advancement rather than out of condescending interest.

Clearly, bureaucratization has increased and relationships are becoming increasingly formalized. Equally clearly, the company is now making a conscious effort to demolish its patronistic coalitions with its Indian employees in order to insure both the single-stranded objective of the company and the "equal and fair" treatment of all employees which is an important aspect of its bureaucratic ideology.

SUMMARY AND CONCLUSION

There appears to be at least a three-phase developmental process in terms of linkages between Copper Corporation and its Papago Indian employees over the years of their dealings with each other. In the first phase, the company as such took relatively little formal interest, and linkages were achieved by means of asymmetrical dyads between Anglo and Papago individuals. At some point in this first phase, however, corporation officials began to be aware of discrepancies between what they expected of Indian employees and what the Indians expected of themselves. The corporation view was that the Indians could not become very good employees as long as they did not demand more of themselves in the way of better living standards, greater sobriety, work dependability, the prudent use of money, and the like.

Company attempts to correct or change some of these conditions by instituting formally planned company service programs marked the beginning of phase two. These included company-controlled rewards and other procedures designed to alter undesirable patterns and activities incompatible with the demands of the company. But at least part of the new structure had to reflect the inherently unequal, asymmetrical nature of the linkage. That is, although the ultimate goal was to upgrade and improve the Indians' status so that their customary patterns would not be too inconsistent with company expectations, it was recognized that dealing with "unequals," who were also "traditionals" called for a degree of condescending patronage until the Indians could become "moderns" in their behavior. To a large extent, the linkage is still in this phase in which the company is changing traditional Papago patterns at the same time it bends its own structure and values to accommodate those patterns.

The final phase is that of complete bureaucratization which calls for treating Indian employees impartially on the basis of their qualifications and not because they are Indians with whom it is necessary to be patient. Copper Corporation is presently ideally committed to this bureaucratic principle, and the anticipated goal is a state in which condescension to particular ethnic groups is no longer necessary and individuals will be hired and dealt with on the basis of their ability to accept and meet the company's performance expectations.

Although the subject is beyond the scope of the present paper, one may ask whether the Indians have acquired any new, nontraditional relationships which might hasten or retard the full attainment of phase three. A minority leadership has in fact emerged within the Indian community and has begun to participate in union activity, press for changing attitudes among their Indian neighbors, and to urge more "equal" treatment of Indians. Yet this same leadership also works to maintain the separate identity of the Indian community and to retain strong identifications with their reservation communities. They resist becoming "made-over" white men, as many think Copper Corporation has been trying to make them. Some of the most able and promising Papago men have therefore resisted the condescending efforts of the company leaders to "help" them be more like white men. Absenteeism, drinking, lack of participation in affairs of the larger community, refusals to participate in union activities, and the rejection of offered promotions appear at times and in part to be efforts at maintaining Indian identity by conforming to institutionalized stereotypes that have developed as a result of these several decades of interaction among Indians, the non-Indian community, and Copper Corporation.

If and when the third phase of the bureaucratization process is completed, the ethnic community as such will no longer exist. This seems to be the goal ideally visualized by Copper Corporation, but the reality of its attainment is delayed as much by the persistence of the Corporation's own condescending structures and stereotyped relationships carried over from the previous two phases as by any cultural behavior that may be peculiar to Papagos or other American Indians.

The case of Copper Corporation is a specific example of a very widespread dilemma in modern society. Both governmental institutions and private businesses and industries are inclined toward reducing the malintegration of various subcultural segments comprising their systems, not only because of increasing benevolent awareness that equal access to the benefits of contemporary life does not exist, but also because the very efficiency and welfare of an industrial society depend upon a reduction of socioeconomic discrepancies between segments. The only way for greater integration of systems to occur appears to be a purposeful building of structures which are intended to facilitate changes that allow for greater participation in the social and economic benefits of a technological society. Yet it appears that it is a very common practice to perpetuate forms of token paternalism whenever bureaucratic egalitarianism does not transpire as planned. Thus, patronage may not only be a temporary interim structure; it may persist as a means of integrating unequal segments over long periods of time and fail to achieve the egalitarian ideal which prompted the initial planning. And, in the process, the socially and economically deprived may either be provided structural support for behaving in ways consistent with patronage and inconsistent with bureaucratic goals, or become increasingly apathetic about participating in the system as it is. In either case, the egalitarian objectives are long delayed and, as a result, human beings are disillusioned as well. Given the preponderance of paternalism maintained in well-intended programs of change, it would seem most crucial to consider whether or not there are other ways of linking unequal segments besides resorting to structures that perpetuate paternalism in the "intermediate" phases. As the case of Copper Corporation reveals, once there is a commitment to condescending patronage in the structure of a program, it may be very difficult to prevent it from becoming something more than an interim means to a final egalitarian goal. It may become a permanent structural linkage.

Introduction to
Community Conflict and the Development of a Worker Elite in a Cali Barrio

In contrast to Suru Lere, people were not forced into the housing project described in this selection; it was eagerly anticipated. Nevertheless, problems and conflicts among residents developed because of the way it was planned. Although different construction plans were made available to applicants, it was planned and serviced as one community—but the differences in the construction plans entailed more sweeping differences in the lives of the residents which, when made visible, resulted in community conflicts.

People who had steady company jobs enjoyed better access to credit and a full range of fringe benefits such as discount shopping, educational subsidies, medical and dental services, and pensions. They had the kind of security, and gave the kind of loyalty, that comes from the special relationship they had with their employers. Residents of the other sector of the barrio tended to have more fluctuating incomes and were excluded from participation in credit unions. As a result they were more dependent on, and integrated with, the local community and looked to it as a source of livelihood, in contrast to the company employees who were more modern, mobile, and regarded themselves more as residents of Cali than of the barrio.

The higher standard of living and greater security the company employees enjoyed was envied by the residents of the self-help sector, so that intracommunity conflict based on cultural differences was aggravated to the point of breakdown of community integration. This case study illustrates how the visibility of discrepancies in economic status can be disruptive to a sense of community. In mixed housing, differences in income can create alienation and disaffection. Any differences in type of facilities available will be perceived as inequalities, especially if they correspond to existing economic inequities. Given the potential people have for feeling deprived in the face of uneven economic development, it is important to avoid creating a sense of relative deprivation by creating structures which emphasize real differences. In the case of this barrio, policies which set out to accommodate cultural and economic diversity ended up penalizing the people who were more marginal to the modernization process as Cali industrialized.

---

17. COMMUNITY CONFLICT AND THE DEVELOPMENT OF A WORKER ELITE IN A CALI BARRIO

by Elizabeth Hegeman

In the summer of 1964, discord had developed between two sectors in a tract of public housing just outside Cali, Colombia, before the project was even finished. The two neighborhoods were already being called by different names—El Guabal and Panamericano—and unfounded rumors were flying that the municipal government was going to divide the barrio and build another community center. In El Guabal, residents were telling each other that the mortgage payments in Panamericano had been canceled, and in Panamericano neighbors buzzed about the shiftless ne'er-do-wells in Guabal who were trying to wring more benefits from the city government. It was reported that during the procession of the duly

This research was supported by the Metropolitan Graduate Summer Field Training Program, sponsored by the Ford Foundation, and administered by the Institute of Latin American Studies at Columbia University.

elected queen of the barrio, stones and soda bottles had been thrown as the parade passed through Panamericano by disgruntled residents who wished to advance their own queen.

Administrators in the community center were perplexed. They had anticipated few problems with the residents, who they thought were largely recent immigrants from rural areas, fleeing from the violence that had decimated the countryside during the previous twelve years. They expected residents to have few social ties of any kind and very little political sophistication. The pattern of invading unused land and building dwellings overnight was widespread throughout Latin America, and the housing project was intended to forestall such invasions by relieving some of the pressure for housing.

Officials of the housing agency were mystified at the dissatisfactions as well—they had thought that in a city where thousands of squatters were crowded into makeshift huts and were buying water from trucks at exorbitant rates, the new residents would be overjoyed at having their own relatively spacious plots, complete with public water, electricity, wide roads, public transport to the downtown area, and their own community center. The Instituto de Crédito Territorial (Institute of Territorial Credit), funded by foreign aid and associated with the Colombian government, had an outstanding record of providing low-cost single-family housing in projects all over the country.

Very little was certain about the conflict but that the two sectors wanted to separate. In an effort to find out some of the causes of the discord, forty interviews were conducted with one family selected randomly from each inhabited block in the housing project, which numbered a thousand families and was still growing. The interviews lasted from an hour to several hours, and were aimed at finding out views of the project, participation in community activities, attitudes toward institutions, economic situation, and life style as well as basic demographic data. Some profound cultural and economic differences between the two sectors emerged from the interviews, which shed light on the conflicts rending the community.

In the attempt to provide for the diverse desires and economic capabilities of families in need of housing, the ICT had offered three different plans to those who applied. The

Incomplete House plan was chosen by families who could afford a higher initial payment, and could allocate a substantial amount of monthly income to pay off their mortgage rapidly. They were provided with a complete cinder-block shell with cement floor, plumbing, and electrical wiring. The Mutual Help plan was chosen by families who could afford a lower initial payment, and wanted to labor themselves in teams to build ten houses to ICT specifications, with materials purchased through the ICT. None of the teams had been able to fulfill their objectives, however; men who were employed in other jobs could not contribute enough time for the houses to be built rapidly, and the original plan to allocate the finished houses by lot among the cooperating families proved unsatisfactory because finished houses would have to stand empty while families were in desperate need. In most cases the ICT construction crews completed these houses according to the Incomplete House plan. The Incomplete House and Mutual Aid sections formed that part of the barrio which called itself Panamericano.

Under both plans housing was completed more quickly and satisfactorily than in the Self Help section of the barrio. Families who could afford a lower initial payment and carrying charges purchased only their lots, and even though interest rates offered were much lower than available elsewhere in the city, these families grumbled at the long time they would have to wait before they would actually have title to their land. Houses in this sector, called El Guabal, were more makeshift, with dirt floors and walls of caned wood; although electrical hookups were available, the houses were sometimes not adequately wired for the connections. Communal showers, latrines, and pumps rather than private plumbing served these homes. The drainage was poor in Guabal and houses near the river suffered seasonal flooding and mosquitoes. Roads had been left unpaved until sewers could be installed, but it was discovered that the water table was too high for pipes to be laid, and the knee-deep mud for three months of the year provided an additional source of dissatisfaction for the residents of Guabal.

In offering the different plans for construction, the ICT had unwittingly established two communities with very different economic bases. These economic differences corresponded to important cultural differences as well, and the combination made for community conflict. The obvious discrepancy in quality of housing, and the proximity of the two homogeneous sectors heightened the visibility of the differences. Since it would not have been difficult to foresee the frictions that developed as a result of the mixed plan, it seems likely that it emerged in response to political pressures from outside the community: AID policies encouraged the construction of high quality housing, while the major pressures on the mayor's office in Cali came from people in desperate need of land, with insufficient resources to pay for "middle-income" housing. Thus the mixed plan was probably a compromise between these two interest groups rather than a result of consultation with future community residents.

While the average family income as revealed in the interviews was 735 pesos per month in Panamericano and 535 pesos per month in Guabal, this difference was offset by barter and small gardens in Guabal. More important, a much higher proportion of heads of families in Panamericano were employed in stable positions with large companies offering fringe benefits and opportunities for credit. Company and union credit rather than savings had allowed these families to make the initial payments to the ICT. In Guabal, however, two-thirds of the residents were self-employed or irregularly employed, and had to expend a higher proportion of their income buying in more expensive local stores in order to build up credit for lean times. These families had to rely on meager savings and current income to meet their payments to the ICT. Employees of large companies had access to cooperative stores where they could make weekly purchases at a discount; often these companies offered educational, medical, and insurance benefits as well.

Use of the community center reflected these differences in economic patterns and life styles as well. Residents of Panamericano had been installed before those in El Guabal. They had initially come in greater numbers to the classes in nutrition and rhythm method of birth control, and had used the clinic and cooperative store. As Guabal became more populated, however, the women from Panamericano began to shun the center commissariat because Caritas (Catholic Charities) distributed free food to indigents from the same place, and they were reluctant to be seen there. The more frequently unemployed residents of Guabal relied more heavily on the distributions of surplus food, and brought their problems to the attention of social workers in the community center. Guabal mothers made more use of the daycare center, as they were more frequently forced by economic circumstances to work. Having no access to company health care, they came to the clinic at the community center more frequently as well.

Residents of Guabal were ambivalent toward the center, despite their greater need and use of it. In a few interviews they expressed anticlerical suspicions, as the Center was funded by a private religious family foundation, and the focus of its activities was the religious calendar. Even more frequently, they expressed the desire not to be obligated to anyone, and the sentiment that the center was dispensing charity. Social workers at the center were uneasy at how long it was taking for residents to become accustomed to using the center, and at the falling-off of participation by residents of Panamericano. They were well aware of the desire of the two communities for separate facilities, but accurately pointed out that the barrio of 15,000 was too small to command two separate sets of municipal services, and since residents still had to come to school and church at the center, people had no choice but to cooperate. The social workers saw the animosities as superficial and expected them to be resolved in time, but the picture emerging from the interviews suggests that the division was a permanent one, based on differences between traditional and modern life-styles.

For example, residents of El Guabal asked neighbors and close relatives to be the godparents of their children, while residents of Panamericano asked superiors on the job or acquaintances in the professions to be compadres. Since the institution of compadrazgo establishes a relationship of mutual help and obligation between the parents and the godparents, having well-placed compadres is a good indicator of ambition and freedom from immediate anxiety over the future of the children. Having compadres close by shows more concern with solidifying already close relationships in case immediate survival is threatened, and is more typical in rural areas of Colombia.

In addition, residents of Panamericano were, at the time of the study, more oriented toward the downtown Cali area than were the residents of Guabal; they were using Panamericano as a "dormitory suburb." They made an average of eight more bus trips per family per week, sent their children to high school and private schools downtown, wore clothes from department stores, and made use of company clinics and stores. In Guabal, people relied much more heavily on local resources, and many homes did double service as seamstress and hairdressing parlors, front room stores and bars. Many small gardens and a few chickens augmented the income of residents, who were less involved in the money economy. They consulted yerbiteras, local herbal healers who could be paid by barter, much more frequently than residents of Panamericano did.

Differences between the communities were reflected in the history of the Community Action juntas. The junta program had been initiated by the Colombian government in the 1950s as a way of encouraging communities to organize improvement programs, and as a way of channeling governmental aid to local areas. Barrio Panamericano had succeeded in going through official channels to incorporate its own Community Action junta, which held weekly meetings and had organized Saturday work crews and borrowed machinery to install sidewalks. The municipality of Cali dissolved the original junta that had been organized by the whole barrio shortly after this secession, because the residents of Guabal did not maintain it. But in Guabal a "pirate" junta, which lacked official recognition, engaged in vigilante activities—for example, when another barrio, on higher ground, began to dump sewage into the river that bordered Guabal, the "pirate" junta made an expedition in the middle of the night to divert the sewage back into the streets of that barrio. These extralegal activities brought prompt municipal attention to the situation, but they confirmed Guabal residents' lack of faith in official channels. Widespread suspicion of authorities was characteristic of the Self-Help sector—the Community Action junta had become defunct because no one was willing to serve on the committee for fear of being accused of taking graft. Thus a very major difference between the two communities was the amount of faith they had in the political process. The "pirate" junta, made up of anonymous members, continued its guerrilla actions by spreading rumors that the municipal government and the ICT were favoring Panamericano with regard to bus routes, terms of loans, and the paving of roads as well as drainage problems. Though the content of the rumors was not true, they expressed the feelings residents of Guabal had of being left out of the modernization process, which was certainly not far from the truth. There were no corresponding rumors in Panamericano because residents did not feel the same kinds of resentments and were less involved generally in the local community. It is remarkable how quickly and thoroughly those who were able to obtain company jobs changed their lives to incorporate benefits, from downtown shopping and service patterns to higher aspirations for their children. The kind of patronage relationship they had with their companies was very different from the traditional relationship they might have experienced with an absentee landlord in the countryside, who confers benefits by whim, and from the charity relationship some families in Guabal were cultivating with the community center. The fringe benefits workers enjoyed were part of the job, and conferred according to impersonal criteria such as length of service. The problems company paternalism created here were not problems for the recipients, but for the morale of the larger community.

Residents of Panamericano and Guabal had lived in Cali for approximately the same length of time—13.6 years and 11.4 years respectively—and there was little evidence that those who held company jobs had had more skills when they were hired. Since they differed so little in urban residence, background, and skills from the "lucky ones," the marginally employed were experiencing a disguised form of class consciousness which crystallized around the different construction plans. They saw quite clearly the advantages of a company job, but felt they had only themselves to blame, so they couldn't express their resentments directly against those who enjoyed company benevolence. Families living in ICT-built homes had indeed received more of a subsidy from the program—they were able to reap the benefits of expertise, efficiency, and economies of scale offered by a modern housing program because they had access to credit—and so the resentments of those who did not benefit as much were directed against the ICT program rather than directly against their more fortunate neighbors.

Painful relative deprivation, as some people benefit more directly from the industrialization process and others continue to live in traditional ways, is a major problem in developing nations just as it is in more industrialized ones. The conflicts and disintegration of a sense of community in El Guabal-Panamericano are a microcosm of this dilemma of modernization, and a lesson to organizations such as the Institute of Territorial Credit and the Community Action programs that efforts aimed at enhancing opportunities can sometimes enhance the inequalities that already exist.

Introduction to
The Changing Values and Institutions of Vicos in the Context of National Development

People assume that development and modernization mean urbanization. The Vicos project provides a model for rural development very attractive to planners in countries where rapid migration brings people into urban centers not equipped to deal with their needs for employment, housing, sanitation, education, public transport. The primary stimulus for migration in many areas is the below subsistence level of rural life and the hope for a better life in the city. The Cornell-Peru project at Vicos is an example of what can be done in a rural area to raise the economic level and increase the satisfactions of life in a farming community.

The essential ingredient for positive change in rural areas in most of the world is land reform. Under the hacienda system land use is controlled by one landlord who requires his tenants to work the plantation in exchange for a small piece of land for their own use. Under this system the worker has no security and all decisions are made at the discretion of the patron. Health and education services are almost nonexistent, and the average worker has no access to any means of improving his options.

By assuming the administration of the hacienda, Cornell-Peru was able to enlist the workers in setting and reaching goals for community development. The explicit aim of the effort was to bring the community to a point of self-government and self-determination so that social change could be sustained even in the absence of outsiders.

For this model to work on a wide scale over any period of time the government of a developing nation must facilitate the transfer of land from private or public ownership to collective. Furthermore, the project must be part of an economic network which ensures access to a market for their produce and protects them from sabotage and exploitation by surrounding hacendados and merchants whose position may be threatened by the success of a cooperative venture.

The development of responsive leadership and the assumption of decision-making powers by the local community are goals for an urban community as well as a rural one. As this happens, those who have been servicing the community solely for profit motives are threatened; landlords, banks, local merchants, and ward politicians will oppose cooperative activity in order to maintain community dependency on them. In order for a community to assume control over its institutions, it is necessary to understand the nature of their economic involvements. Self government is important for community development but it is also necessary to develop techniques that deal with economic coercion and manipulation as the Vicosinos managed to deal with pressure from the Mestizos and others interested in perpetuating dependency.

18. THE CHANGING VALUES AND INSTITUTIONS OF VICOS IN THE CONTEXT OF NATIONAL DEVELOPMENT

by Allan R. Holmberg

More than 50 per cent of the world's population is peasantry, the large majority of whom are living in the so-called underdeveloped countries or newly emerging nations under natural conditions and social structures that have denied them effective participation in the modernization process. In the context

From *American Behavioral Scientist*, Volume 8, No. 7, March 1965, pp. 3–8.

of a modern state, this peasantry plays little or no role in the decision-making process; its members enjoy little access to wealth; they live under conditions of social disrespect; a large majority of them are illiterate, unenlightened, and lacking in modern skills; many are victims of ill health and disease. Characteristic of this sector of the world's population is a deep devotion to magico-religious practice as a means of mitigating the castigations of a harsh and cruel world over which it has little or no control. Such, in fact, were the conditions of life on the *Hacienda Vicos*, a community which is the subject of this paper.

Operating on the assumption that these conditions of human indignity are not only anachronistic in the modern world but are also a great threat to public and civic order everywhere, Cornell University, in 1952—in collaboration with the Peruvian Indianist Institute—embarked on an experimental program of induced technical and social change which was focused on the problem of transforming one of Peru's most unproductive, highly dependent manor systems into a productive, independent, self-governing community adapted to the reality of the modern Peruvian state.

Up until January 1952, Vicos was a manor or large estate, situated in a relatively small intermontane valley of Peru, about 250 miles north of the capital city of Lima. Ranging in altitude from about 9,000 to 20,000 feet, Vicos embraced an area of about 40,000 acres and had an enumerated population of 1,703 monolingual Quechua-speaking Indians who had been bound to the land as serfs or peons since early colonial times.

Vicos was a public manor, a type not uncommon in Peru. Title to such properties is frequently held by Public Benefit or Charity Societies which rent them out to the highest bidder at public auction for periods ranging from five to ten years. Each such manor has particular lands, usually the most fertile bottom lands, reserved for commercial exploitation by the successful renter who utilizes, virtually free of charge for several days of each week, the serf-bound labor force, usually one adult member of every family, to cultivate his crops. The rent from the property paid to the Public Benefit Society is supposed to be used for charitable purposes, such as the sup-

port of hospitals and other welfare activities, although this is
not always the case. Under the contractual arrangements between the renter and the Public Benefit Society (and sometimes the indigenous population) the former is legally but not
always functionally bound to supply, in return for the labor
tax paid by his serfs, plots of land (usually upland) of sufficient size to support the family of each inscribed peon.

Manors like Vicos are socially organized along similar lines.
At the head of the hierarchy stands the renter or *patrón*,
frequently absentee, who is always an outsider and non-Indian
or Mestizo. He is the maximum authority within the system
and all power to indulge or deprive is concentrated in his
hands. Under his direction, if absentee, is an administrator,
also an outsider and Mestizo, who is responsible to the renter
for conducting and managing the day-to-day agricultural or
grazing operations of the property. Depending on the size of
the manor, the administrator may employ from one to several
Mestizo foremen who are responsible for the supervision of
the labor force. They report directly to the administrator on
such matters as the number of absentee members of the labor
force, and the condition of the crops regarding such factors
as irrigation, fertilization, and harvest.

Below and apart from this small non-Indian power elite
stands the Indian society of peons, the members of which
are bound to a soil they do not own and on which they have
little security of tenure. The direct link between the labor
force and the administration is generally through a number of
Indian straw bosses, appointed by the *patrón* and responsible
for the direct supervision of the labor force in the fields. Each
straw boss or *Mayoral*, as he was known at Vicos, had under
his direction a certain number of *peones* from a particular
geographic area of the manor. In 1952 there were eight straw
bosses at Vicos, with a total labor force of about 380 men. In
addition to the labor tax paid by the Indian community, its
members were obligated to supply other free services to the
manor such as those of cooks, grooms, swineherds, watchmen,
and servants. The whole system is maintained by the application of sanctions ranging from brute force to the impounding
of peon property.

In matters not associated directly with manor operations,

the Indian community of Vicos was organized along separate and traditional lines. The principal indigenous decision-making body consisted of a politico-religious hierarchy of some seventeen officials known as *Varas* or *Varayoc,* so named from the custom of carrying a wooden staff as a badge of office. The major functions of this body included the settling of disputes over land and animals in the Indian community, the supervision of public works such as the repair of bridges and the community church, the regulation of marriage patterns, and the celebration of religious festivals. The leading official in this hierarchy was the *Alcalde* or mayor who assumed office, after many years of service to the community, by a kind of elective system and who occupied it for only one year. The *Varayoc* were the principal representatives of the Indian community to the outside world.

In 1952 all Vicosinos were virtual subsistence farmers, occupying plots of land ranging in size from less than one-half to about five acres. The principal crops raised were maize, potatoes and other Andean root crops, wheat, barley, rye, broad beans, and quinoa. In addition, most families grazed some livestock (cattle, sheep, goats, and swine) and all families raised small animals like guinea pigs and chickens as a way of supplementing their diets and their incomes. After thousands of years of use and inadequate care, however, the land had lost its fertility, seeds had degenerated, and the principal crops and animals were stunted and diseased. Per capita output was thus at a very low level, although the exact figure is not known.

In addition, many Vicosinos suffered from malnutrition; most were victims of a host of endemic diseases. Studies in parasitology demonstrated that 80 per cent of the population was infected with harmful parasites, and epidemics of such diseases as measles and whooping cough had been frequent over the years. There were, to be sure, native curers employing magico-religious practices and ineffectual herbal remedies to cope with these well-being problems but it can be said that the community had little or no access to modern medicine. The goal of the traditional Vicosino was simply to survive as long as he possibly could, knowing full well that he might be a victim of fate at any moment.

The principal avenue for gaining respect in traditional Vicos society was to grow old and to participate in the politico-religious hierarchy, the top positions of which could be occupied only after many years of faithful service to the community. Wealth was also a source of gaining prestige and recognition but it could not be amassed in any quantity, by native standards, until one's elders had died or until an individual himself had lived frugally and worked very hard for many years. In other words, the principal role to which high rank was attached was that of a hard-working, muscle-bound, virtual subsistence farmer who placed little or no value on other occupations or skills. Consequently there was just no place for a rebellious or symbolically creative individual in traditional Vicos society. The manor system was, of course, in large part responsible for this. It needed few skills beyond brawn, and enlightenment could not be tolerated, because the more informed the population, the more it might become a threat to the traditional manor system. Records show that all protest movements at Vicos had been pretty much squelched by a coalition of the landlords, the clergy, and the police. As a result, over a period of several hundred years the community had remained in static equilibrium and was completely out of step with anything that was occurring in the modern world. The rule at Vicos was conformity to the status quo. It pervaded all institutions and dominated the social process. The peon was subservient to the overlord; the child, to the parents; and both were beaten into submission. Even the supernatural forces were punishing, and the burdens one bore were suffered as naturally ordained by powers beyond one's control.

INTERVENTION FROM WITHOUT

The Cornell Peru Project intervened in this context in 1952 in the role of *patrón*. Through a partly fortuitous circumstance—the industrial firm which was renting Vicos on a ten-year lease that still had five years to run went bankrupt—we were able to sublease the property and its serfs for a five-year period. For a couple of years prior to this time, however, the Peruvian anthropologist, Dr. Mario Vazquez, had conducted a very detailed study of this manor as a social system, as part of a larger comparative study of modernization of peasant societies that the Department of Anthropology at Cornell was conducting in several areas of the world. Thus when the opportunity to rent the *hacienda* arose, we seized upon it to conduct our own experiment in modernization. In its negotiations prior to renting the *hacienda*, Cornell received full support of the Peruvian Government through its Institute of Indigenous Affairs, a semi-autonomous agency of the Ministry of Labor and Indigenous Affairs. In December 1951, a formal Memorandum of Agreement was drawn up between Cornell and the Institute of Indigenous Affairs, and the Cornell Peru Project became a reality at Vicos on January 1, 1952.

Several months prior to assuming the responsibilities of the power role at Vicos, a plan of operations was drawn up which was focused on the promotion of human dignity rather than indignity and the formation of institutions at Vicos which would allow for a wide rather than a narrow shaping and sharing of values for all the participants in the social process. The principal goals of this plan thus became the devolution of power to the community, the production and broad sharing of greater wealth, the introduction and diffusion of new and modern skills, the promotion of health and well being, the enlargement of the status and role structure, and the formation of a modern system of enlightenment through schools and other media. It was hoped that by focusing on institutions specialized to these values as independent variables this would also have some modernizing effect on the more dependent variables, namely, the institutions specialized to affection (family and kinship) and rectitude (religion and ethics), which are sensitive areas of culture in which it is generally more hazardous to intervene directly.

In designing our program and a method of strategic intervention, we were very much aware of two, among many, guiding principles stemming from anthropological research: first, innovations are most likely to be accepted in those aspects of culture in which people themselves feel the greatest deprivations; and second, an integrated or contextual approach to value-institutional development is usually more lasting and less conflict-producing than a piecemeal one. Consequently, we established our operational priorities on the basis of the first principle but tried to optimize change in all areas at the same time, realizing, of course, that with scarce resources, all values could not be maximized concurrently. Perhaps a few examples will best illustrate our use of the method of strategic intervention.

Our first entry into more than a research role at Vicos coincided with a failure of the potato harvest of both the *patrón* and the serf community due to a blight which had attacked the crop. The poor of the community were literally starving, and even the rich were feeling the pinch. Complaints about the theft of animals and food were rife. At the same time, previous study of the manor had enlightened us about the major gripes of the serfs against the traditional system. These turned out not to be such things as the major commitment of each head of household to contribute one peon to the labor force for three days of each week, but the obligation of the Indian households to supply the extra, free services to the manor previously mentioned. Since we were in a position of power, it was relatively easy to abolish these services. A decision was made to do so, and volunteers were hired to perform these jobs for pay. Thus an immediate positive reinforcement was supplied to the community in our power relationship with it.

An added incentive to collaborate with the new administration resulted from the fact that we as *patrones* reimbursed the serfs for labor which they had performed under the previous administration but for which they had not been paid for approximately three years. Under the traditional system, each peon was entitled to about three cents per week for the work performed under the labor tax. In some Peruvian manors this is paid in the form of coca leaves, which most adult males chew, but at Vicos it was supposed to have been paid in cash. By deducting the back pay from the cost of the transfer of the manor to our control, we fulfilled earlier commitments, with the money of the previous administration, and received the credit for it. Through such small but immediately reinforcing interventions, a solid base for positive relations with members of the community was first established. In this regard, of course, we were greatly aided by Dr. Vazquez, who had previously spent almost two years in the community, living with an Indian family, and who personally knew, and was trusted by almost every one of its members.

INCREASING AGRICULTURAL PRODUCTIVITY

As mentioned above, one of the most immediate and urgent tasks at Vicos was to do something about its failing economy which, in reality, meant increasing its agricultural productivity. Manors like Vicos are never productive because the renter during his period of tenure puts as little as possible into the operation and exploits the property for as much as he possibly can. The serfs, on the other hand, make no improvements on their lands, or other capital investments, because they, too, have no security of tenure. As a consequence, most such manors are in a very bad state of repair.

Since the Cornell Peru Project possessed funds only for research and not for capital development, the wealth base had to be enlarged by other capital means. It was decided, in consultation with Indian leaders, who were early informed about the goals of the Project, that no major changes would be initiated immediately in the day-to-day operations of the manor. We even retained the former Mestizo administrator, a close friend of the Project Director and Field Director, who agreed to reorient his goals to those of the Project.

The principal resources available to the Project were the labor of the Indian community and the lands which had been formerly farmed by the overlord. By employing this labor to farm these lands by modern methods (the introduction of fertilizer, good seed, pesticides, proper row spacing, etc.), and by growing marketable food crops, capital was accumulated for enlarging the wealth base. Returns from these lands, instead of being removed from the community, as was the case under the traditional system, were plowed back into the experiment to foment further progress towards our goals. Profits from the Project's share of the land were not only employed further to improve agricultural productivity but also to construct health and educational facilities, to develop a wider range of skills among the Indian population, and to reconstruct what had been a completely abandoned administrative center of operations. At the same time, new techniques of potato production and other food crops, first demonstrated on Project lands, were introduced to the Indian households which, within a couple of years, gave a sharp boost to the Indian economy. In short, by 1957 when Cornell's lease on the land expired, a fairly solid economic underpinning for the whole operation had been established, and the goal of considerably enlarging the wealth base had been accomplished.

DEVOLUTION OF POWER

From the very first day of operations, we initiated the process of power devolution. It was decided that it would be impossible to work with the traditional *Varas* as a leadership group, because they were so occupied during their terms of office with religious matters that they would have no time to spend on secular affairs. On the other hand, the former straw bosses, all old and respected men, had had a great deal of direct experience in conducting the affairs of the manor for the *patrón*. It was decided not to bypass this group even though we knew that its members had enjoyed the greatest indulgences under the traditional system and, being old, would be less likely to be innovative than younger men. Under prevailing conditions, however, this seemed to be the best alternative to pursue. As it turned out, it proved to be an effective transitional expedient. Gradually, as success was achieved in the economic field, it became possible to replace (by appointment) the retiring members of this body with younger men more committed to the goals of modernization. For instance, men finishing their military service, an obligation we encouraged them to fulfill, returned home with at least an exposure to other values and institutions in Peruvian society. In pre-Cornell days such returning veterans were forced back in the traditional mold within a few days time, with no opportunity to give expression to any newly found values they may have acquired. Insofar as possible, we tried to incorporate people of this kind into decision-making bodies and tried to provide them opportunities to practice whatever new skills they had acquired. In the first five years of the Project, not only did age composition of the governing body completely change, but decision-making and other skills had developed to a point where responsibility for running the affairs of the community was largely in indigenous hands. A complete transfer of power took place in 1957, when a council of ten delegates, and an equal number of subdelegates, was elected to assume responsibility for community affairs. This council, elected annually, has performed this function ever since.

In the area of well-being it was much more difficult to devise a strategy of intervention that would show immediate and dramatic pay-off. This is a value area, to be sure, in which great deprivation was felt at Vicos, but it is also one in which the cooperation of all participants in the community was necessary in order to make any appreciable impact on it. The major well-being problems at Vicos, even today, stem from public health conditions. All individuals are deeply concerned about their personal well-being but are unwilling to forego other value indulgences to make this a reality for the community as a whole. Nor were the resources available to do so at the time the Project began.

A variety of attempts was made to tackle the most urgent health problems. In collaboration with the Peruvian Ministry of Health and Social Welfare, a mobile clinic was started at Vicos, which made at least one visit to the community each week. Support for this effort came from the community itself in the form of the construction of a small sanitary post at which the sick could be treated. It was hoped to staff this clinic through the Public Health services of Peru, but all attempts to do so were frustrated by lack of budget and responsibly trained personnel. In Peru, such services seldom extend into rural areas because the preferred values of the medical profession are, as almost everywhere, associated with city life. Consequently, no major public health effort was launched and the community's state of well-being has shown little net gain. What gains have been made stem principally from improved nutrition, but as enlightenment about the germ theory of disease diffuses and the results of modern medicine are clearly demonstrated, through the application of public health measures that take native beliefs into account, we expect a sharp rise in the well-being status of the community to follow.

OPTIMIZING GOALS

Strategies for optimizing Project goals for the respect, affection, and rectitude values, first rested heavily on the examples set by Project personnel. From the very beginning, for example, an equality of salutation was introduced in all dealings with the Vicosinos; they were invited to sit down at the tables with us; there was no segregation allowed at public affairs; Project personnel lived in Indian houses. At the same time, we attempted to protect the constitutional rights of Vicosinos, which had been previously flagrantly violated by the Mestizo world. Abuses by Mestizo authorities and army recruiters were no longer tolerated. The draft status of all Vicosinos was regularized; they were encouraged to fulfill their legal obligations to the nation. While not directly intervening in the family, or tampering with religious practice, the indirect effect of optimizing other values on the respect position of the community soon became evident. As Vicosinos mastered modern techniques of potato production, for example, they were approached by their Mestizo compatriots in the surrounding area, seeking advice as to how to improve their crops.

Even the rectitude patterns at Vicos began to change. When we first took control of the manor, rates of theft were extremely high. Every peon farmer, as his crops were maturing, had to keep watchmen in his fields at night. As the Indian economy rose and starvation was eliminated, this practice disappeared completely. Even the parish priest became an enthusiastic supporter of the Project. His services were more in demand, to say nothing of their being much better paid.

A strategy of promoting enlightenment at Vicos was initiated through the adaptation of a traditional manor institution to goals and values of the Project. In most Andean manors run along the lines of Vicos, the peons, after completing their three days labor, must report to the manor house where they receive their work orders for the following week. This session of all peons, straw bosses, and the *patrón* is known as the *mando*. We devised a strategy of meeting the day before the *mando* with the *mayorales* or decision-making body and utilizing the *mando* to communicate and discuss the decisions taken. Since heads of all households were present, the *mando* provided an excellent forum for the communication of news, the discussion of plans, progress towards goals, etc.

A long-run strategy of enlightenment rested on the founding of an educational institution at Vicos that could provide continuity for Project goals, training of leadership dedicated to the process of modernization, and the formation of a wide range of skills. Through collaboration with the Peruvian Ministry of Education and the Vicos community itself, this became a possibility. Within the period of Cornell's tenure, levels of enlightenment and skill rose sharply and their effects have been substantial throughout the society.

TRANSFER OF TITLE

In 1957, at the time Cornell's lease in Vicos expired, the Project made a recommendation to the Peruvian Government, through its Institute of Indigenous Affairs, to expropriate the property from the holders of the title, the Public Benefit Society of Huaraz, in favor of its indigenous inhabitants. By this time we felt that a fairly solid value institutional base, with the goals of modernization that we had originally formulated, had been established in the community. The Peruvian Government acted upon the recommendation and issued a decree of expropriation.

It was at this point that the experiment became especially significant, both in the local area and throughout the nation, for national development. Prior to this time, although considerable favorable national publicity had been given to the Project, little attention had been paid to it by the local power elite, except in terms of thinking that the benefits of the developments that had taken place would eventually revert to the title holders. It was inconceivable in the local area that such a property might be sold back to its indigenous inhabitants. Consequently, local power elites immediately threw every possible legal block in the way of the title reverting to the Indian community. They set a price on the property that would have been impossible for the Indian community ever to pay; members of the Project were charged with being agents of the communist world; the Vicosinos were accused of being pawns of American capitalism; Peruvian workers in the field were regarded as spies of the American government. Even such a "progressive" organization as the Rotary Club of Huaraz roundly denounced the Project, accusing its field director of being an agent of communism.

Fortunately, the Project had strong support in the intellectual community of the capital and among many of Peru's agencies of government. The co-director of the Project and President of the Indigenous Institute of Peru (also an internationally recognized scholar in high altitude biology), Dr. Carlos Monge M., was tireless in his effort to see justice done to the Vicosinos. But even his efforts did not bear fruit until almost five years had passed. The reason for this was that not only were the legal blocks of the resistance formidable, but the central government of Peru at this time was an elite government, which, while giving great lip service to the cause of the Vicosinos, was reluctant to take action in their favor. It is a matter of record that many high officials of government were themselves *hacendados*, hesitant to alter the status quo. Consequently, they were able to delay final settlement.

Meanwhile the Vicosinos, now renting the manor directly, were reluctant to develop Vicos because of the danger of their not being able to enjoy the fruits of their labor. While agricultural production rose through the stimulation of a loan from the Agricultural Bank of Peru, other capital investments were not made because of the fear that the price of the property would rise with every investment made. Finally, through pressure exerted by the President of the Institute of Indigenous Affairs and U.S. government officials in Peru, an agreement was reached between the Public Benefit Society and the Vicos community for the direct sale of the property to the Vicosinos at a price and on terms that they could realistically pay. Thus, after a five-year wait following the devolution of power, the community actually became independent in July 1962. Since that time Cornell has played largely a research, advisory, and consultant role, although the Peruvian National Plan of Integration of the Indigenous Populations has had an official government program of development at Vicos since Cornell relinquished control in 1957.

RESULTS

What can be said in a general way about results of the Vicos experience so far? In the first place, if one criterion of a modern democratic society is a parity of power and other values among individuals, then vast gains have been made at Vicos during the past decade. Starting from the base of a highly restrictive social system in which almost all power and other value positions were ascribed and very narrowly shared, the Vicosinos have gradually changed that social system for a much more open one in which all value positions can be more widely shared and they can be attained through achievement. This in itself is no mean accomplishment, particularly since it was done by peaceful and persuasive means.

In the second place, the position of the Vicos community itself, vis-à-vis the immediately surrounding area and the nation as a whole, has undergone a profound change. Starting at the bottom of the heap, and employing a strategy of wealth production for the market place and enlightenment for its people, the community of Vicos has climbed to a position of power and respect that can no longer be ignored by the Mestizo world. This is clearly indexed by the large number of equality relationships which now exist at Vicos (and in inter-community relationships between Vicos and the world outside), where none existed before.

Finally, of what significance is Vicos in the context of national development? Peru is a country with a high degree of unevenness in its development. The highly productive agricultural coast, with off-shore fishing grounds that are among the richest in the world, is moving ahead at a modern and rapid pace. In contrast, the overpopulated sierra, containing major concentrations of indigenous populations, many of whom live under a medieval type agricultural organization, such as exists at Vicos, is lagging far behind. The major lesson of Vicos, for Peru as a whole, is that its serf and suppressed peasant populations, once freed and given encouragement, technical assistance and learning, can pull themselves up by their own bootstraps and become productive citizens of the nation. It is encouraging to see that the present Peruvian Government is taking steps in the right direction. Its programs of land reform and Cooperation Popular may go a long way towards a more peaceful and rapid development of the country as a whole.

SUGGESTED READINGS

Alinsky, Saul D. *Rules For Radicals*. New York: Vintage Books, 1971

Altshuler, Alan A. *Community Control: The Black Demand for Participation in Large American Cities*. New York: Pegasus, 1970

Arensberg, Conrad and Kimball, S. T. *Culture and Community*. New York: Harcourt, Brace & World, 1965

Bellush, Jewel and Hausknecht, Murray, eds. *Urban Renewal: People, Politics and Planning*. Garden City, N.Y.: Anchor Books, 1967

Cahill, Susan and Cooper, Michelle F., eds. *The Urban Reader*. Englewood Cliffs, N.J.: Prentice-Hall, 1971

Clinard, Marshall B. *Slums and Community Development*. New York: The Free Press, 1966

Fava, Sylvia Fleiss, ed. *Urbanism in World Perspective: A Reader*. New York: Thomas Y. Crowell Company, 1968

Foster, George. *Traditional Cultures and the Impact of Technological Change*. New York: Harper & Row, 1962

Gans, Herbert J. *People and Plans: Essays on Urban Problems and Solutions*. New York: Basic Books, 1968

Goodman, Emily Jane. *The Tenant Survival Book*. Indianapolis: The Bobbs-Merrill Co., 1972

Henry, Jules. *Culture Against Man*. New York: Random House, 1963

———. *Pathways to Madness*. New York: Random House, 1971

Hobsbawm, Eric J. *Primitive Rebels: Studies in Archaic Forms of Social Movements in the 19th and 20th Centuries*. New York: W. W. Norton & Company, 1965

Hunnius, Gerry, Garson, G. David, and Case, John, eds. *Workers' Control: A Reader on Labor and Social Change*. New York: Vintage Books, 1973

Jacobs, Jane. *The Death and Life of Great American Cities*. New York: Random House, 1961

Journal of Applied Behavioral Science, Volume 9, Nos. 2/3, 1973, "Alternative Institutions: a Special Issue"

Kotler, Milton. *Neighborhood Government*. Indianapolis: The Bobbs-Merrill Co., 1969

Kuper, Hilda, ed. *Urbanization and Migration in West Africa.* Berkeley: University of California Press, 1965

Leacock, Eleanor Burke, ed. *The Culture of Poverty: A Critique.* New York: Simon and Schuster, 1971

Mangin, William, ed. *Peasants and Cities: Readings in the Anthropology of Urbanization.* Boston: Houghton Mifflin Company, 1970

Marris, Peter and Rein, Martin. *Dilemmas of Social Reform.* Chicago: Aldine Publishing Company, 1967

Miner, Horace. *The City in Modern Africa.* New York: Praeger Publishers, 1967

Oppenheimer, Martin. *The Urban Guerrilla.* Chicago: Quadrangle Books, 1969

Oppenheimer, Martin and Lakey, George. *A Manual for Direct Action.* Chicago: Quadrangle Books, 1964

Phelps, Edmund S. *Private Wants and Public Needs.* New York: W. W. Norton & Company, 1965

Roach, Jack L. and Roach, Janet K., eds. *Poverty.* Baltimore: Penguin Books, 1972

Rodwin, Lloyd. *Nations and Cities.* Boston: Houghton Mifflin Company, 1970

Spradley, James P. and McCurdy, David W., eds. *Conformity and Conflict.* Boston: Little, Brown and Company, 1971

Valentine, Charles A. *Culture and Poverty.* Chicago: University of Chicago Press, 1968

Wirth, Louis. *Community Life and Social Policy: Selected Papers by Louis Wirth,* ed. by Elizabeth Wirth Marvick and Albert J. Reiss, Jr. Chicago: University of Chicago Press, 1966

Zimmerman, Joseph F. *The Federated City: Community Control in Large Cities.* New York: St. Martin's Press, 1972

Index